Edgewise?

Edgewise?

Experiences of some Anglican lay women

Edited by Hannah Ward
and Jennifer Wild

DARTON · LONGMAN + TODD

First published in Great Britain in 2021 by
Darton, Longman and Todd Ltd
1 Spencer Court
140–142 Wandsworth High Street
London SW18 4JJ

ISBN: 978-1-913657-26-0

A catalogue record for this book is available from the British Library.

Designed and produced by Judy Linard

Printed and bound in Great Britain by Bell & Bain, Glasgow

Contents

Contributors

Janet Batsleer has lived in the same house in Manchester for more than thirty years and has worshipped at Holy Innocents Church, Fallowfield, for almost as long.

Margaret Beetham retired some years ago from her academic post in the Department of English at Manchester Metropolitan University and a subsequent Senior Research Fellowship in the School of Arts and Media, at the University of Salford, Manchester. Her most recent publication is *Home is Where: The Journeys of a Missionary Child* (Darton, Longman and Todd, 2019). She lives in Manchester and worships at the Church of the Holy Innocents, Fallowfield, in that city.

Caroline (Caro) Barker Bennett was born in Limpsfield, Surrey, in 1944. She read English at Cambridge and taught English for four years before, first, running a youth and community centre at the Church of the Holy Spirit, Clapham, and then working for a Council of Churches youth project in Oxted and Limpsfield. Her chapter describes where life took her after that.

Maggie Butcher has been a teacher, university lecturer and education administrator, working in Leeds, Nigeria, Canada and London. She worked at the Commonwealth Institute and for

United World Colleges. Her last job before early retirement in 2000 was Academic Registrar at Gresham College in the City of London.

Margaret Halsey was born in Southall, opposite the Quaker Oats factory. Her chapter describes her education in the south of England and student and working life in Scotland, the Midlands, Brighton, South Yorkshire, Manchester and Leeds. In retirement, she has valued the opportunity for swimming and regular exercise in her local leisure centre, started to learn how to draw and paint, enjoyed creative writing, travelled more extensively, and spent more quality time with friends, family and her house rabbit.

Frances Killick qualified as a medical social worker and worked in London and Philadelphia. Later she held a diocesan social responsibility post before freelancing, mainly with clergy and church-related groups, and taking an MSc in gender, society and culture.

Helen Stanton is a Catholic Anglican lay woman. She currently works in the Centre for Ministerial Formation at the Queen's Foundation for Ecumenical Theological Education, Birmingham, where she also teaches spirituality, doctrine and ethics.

Hannah Ward lives and works in Oxfordshire. With her partner, Jennifer Wild, she has written and edited a number of books, including *Human Rites: Worship Resources for an Age of Change* (Mowbray, 1995), *The Monastic Way* (Canterbury Press, 2006) and *Rhythms of Remembering: An Everyday Office Book* (SPCK, 2013).

Jennifer Wild's life falls into three parts, starting with growing up and being educated in New Zealand and (later) England; going on to become and live as a member of a Franciscan religious community; and for the past thirty-odd years writing, editing, gardening and living in partnership with Hannah Ward.

The other three members of the Lay Women's Group were Yvonne Craig Inskip, Sue Parks and Bridget Rees.

1.
Not where we go but who we are

Hannah Ward and Jennifer Wild

The title of this introductory chapter is taken from Maggie Butcher's essay in this collection, which she ends with the reflection 'that church isn't necessarily, or even at all, a place where we go but rather who we are'. It's hardly a new definition of church, but one, as Maggie says, that has been driven home to us in a time of locked churches due to the COVID-19 pandemic. When we set out to work on this project, we didn't know we would be writing while in 'lockdown', trying to talk to each other on Zoom, wondering when we would meet again in the flesh.

So who are we, and why this book?

We've been members of a group of Anglican lay women who have met once a year for the last twenty years. When we've all been able to gather for our annual weekend, there have been twelve of us – a sort of 'cell group' (though some members fiercely resist this description). A year ago we decided to stop meeting before we all got too old or frail to travel (we are based in Northumbria, Manchester, Leeds, London, Exeter, Birmingham and rural Oxfordshire, Wiltshire and West Yorkshire). Nine of us decided we'd like to write something of our stories. Although two names appear as editors on the cover of the book, the process of writing it has been a truly collaborative effort and the editorial process of drafting and revising has been one that has involved all the contributors. Although the three members of the Lay Women's Group who chose not to write for this book haven't been part of that immediate process, we are all aware of how much over the years they have contributed to the ideas and reflections developed in the essays here.

The Lay Women's Group (as we've decided to refer to ourselves in this book – with capital letters) first met in June 2000. It was instigated by Hannah Ward and Jennifer Wild, who sent an invitation to some fellow Anglican lay women. Their letter explained:

> For some time we have been aware, through conversation with friends, that quite a few of us are thinking hard about what it means to be a lay woman in the Church of England now that ordination is an option. Snippets of such conversation, always too brief but always interesting, have made us think that we would like to gather a group together just to see where we are as women committed to being 'lay'. We don't have any fixed agenda, or any thoughts of future dates/events/plans. It will not be an intentionally 'representative' group – we are sending this invitation to friends (in one or two cases, friends of friends).

An initial group of eight met in that first year, and others were invited to join the group for the following year, when we became twelve.

Our meetings have always been over a weekend, from Friday afternoon until after lunch on Sunday. The pattern of gathering has been pretty informal, shaping a loose agenda as we've gone along. We've celebrated and moaned about being part of the church, but we've spent much time talking more broadly about our lives, our work, what it means to give up paid work, about our families, and of course the state of the world and our place in it – and what all this means in the light of the Gospel.

We have always met at the Old Parsonage in Oxfordshire, the convent guest house of the Anglican Community of St Clare, and are immensely grateful for their welcome and generous hospitality. Having the house to ourselves meant that we were able to continue our conversations over meals together as well as in our slightly more formal gatherings.

As a group of women, there are ways in which we're quite a diverse lot, and ways in which we aren't. We're all white, pretty middle-class, between the ages of 62 and 87, and, of course, Anglican and lay. But in other ways we are quite a mixed bunch, with rather different histories and relationships to the church. That diversity is certainly expressed in this book.

The essays here represent our reflecting together and individually on what it's meant to be a lay woman in the church – or, at times, not part of the church. We have discussed together what we have written, but these are our own stories and they express both real diversity and shared experience.

Part of that diversity led to a somewhat extended discussion about the title of this book. Some see themselves as 'on the edge' and happily so, whereas others want to claim the centre ground and are wary of anything that might imply not being fully a part of the church. Others again might use the label 'boundary-dweller' or the description of being liminal. It is certainly not our intention to imply that lay Christians belong in an any less central way than ordained members of the church. But words like 'edge', 'boundary', 'liminal' do say something about being outward-facing, free at least to some degree of institutional responsibility and accountability, and perhaps in a position to engage in the kind of translation Janet Batsleer refers to in her essay.

We are not all English-born – Jennifer is from New Zealand (two other members of the group, who don't have essays in this collection, were born in Australia and Jerusalem). Churchgoing may or may not have been part of our childhood. Some of us have been active churchgoers for most of our lives, others have come and gone and come back again. It's interesting to see how important SCM (Student Christian Movement) has been, and the influence of some strong lay women of a previous generation who acted as role models and theological educators: Mollie Batten in Maggie Butcher's case, Celia Goodenough in Caro Barker Bennett's, for example. Not to mention mothers, grandmothers and great-grandmothers.

Where we have placed ourselves in relation to the church, whether a local church or the national church, also varies. Some of us have spent much of our working lives in the paid employment of the church, in clearly defined roles: in industrial mission, theological education, youth work, pastoral care. Two of us have spent time in religious orders – identifiably 'churchy' perhaps, though neither a clear role nor paid. Other members of the group have worked in the secular world, sometimes in situations where, at best, the church and Christianity generally were regarded with a mixture of suspicion, irrelevance or even outright hostility. Sometimes particular jobs have given opportunity for relationships with those we would otherwise never have met, as in Caro Barker Bennett's work with women in the factories of Tyneside. We represent, in the categories used later by Helen Stanton, Laity A and Laity B.

We've all had a lot of contact with 'not-church', with a world beyond the church – we haven't lived in the kind of church bubble that is often the lot of the clergy. Janet Batsleer, in particular, recognises a role as translator, and sometimes mediator, bridging the different worlds occupied by those she meets and works with; a translation not just of language but of other aspects of culture. The task of translation also has its more obvious place in congregations (at least three mentioned in this book) that have grown through the presence of asylum seekers and refugees.

Liturgy is both language and user of language. While liturgy is mentioned by several authors as a vital, life-giving, part of their Christian life, its limited and patriarchal language is also a cause of frustration and, at times, alienation. It is perhaps fair to say that with the ordination of women to the priesthood it was hoped a more inclusive language might develop. If that is happening, it's happening very slowly. Yes, the language to describe human beings has become more inclusive, but the church's official liturgies still fail to make use of a rich and inclusive language to describe and address God. At different times over the years, many of the members of this group have been part of small liturgy groups, often within established Christian feminist networks like Women in Theology (WIT) and Catholic Women's Network (CWN). Not only do such groups offer opportunities for using more inclusive and creative language, but also for designing rituals, often of transition, that aren't found in the church's prayer books. Margaret Halsey, in her essay, mentions the importance of one such group at times of change in her own life.

The 'language' of silence also features in a number of the essays that follow. Clearly something of value, silence isn't always easy to find in the institutional church. Jennifer Wild found it with the Franciscans in Cambridge and then in a contemplative community; Frances Killick discovered the silent waiting of the Quakers; Margaret Beetham and Janet Batsleer join others in quiet days at their parish church; Helen Stanton alludes to it when she speaks of darkness and vulnerability.

Liturgy groups, feminist theology groups, campaigning groups have all offered what some of the contributors to this volume have described as spaces to the side of the church where exploration and questioning is encouraged, where demands of commitment are much lighter, where the spirit feels generally more free to roam. Paradoxically, it seems such groups are often what sustain a commitment to stay with the church, or even provide a way back to belonging within a church congregation. Many of these groups are specifically Christian; the essay by Hannah Ward describes one such group – Womenspace – which defined itself more broadly. It does, however, share the quality of liminality mentioned in several of the essays, a place of boundary-dwelling and the sort of companionship spoken of by Frances Killick.

It's not surprising considering our age group that there's a fair amount of reference to the feminist movement of the 1970s, to marching and shouting, and days spent at Greenham Common. For some of us, the women's movement of that time took us further from the church; for others, feminism provided a language and companionship to attempt a radical theological and liturgical transformation – a kind of revolutionary project that kept us going. One of the underlying questions of the book is about what happened to all that energy. The usual answer is that it was taken into the institutional church with the ordination of women and into the academy with the rise of feminist theological studies. We seem to be suggesting here, perhaps, that there is still a need for small groups to meet on the margins.

Many of the movements we belonged to in the 1970s and 80s were concerned with aspects of social justice. And this continues to be a common thread in our reflections and something at the heart of what it means for us as lay women. Whether it's as an aspect of our paid employment in the church (as an industrial missioner, educator, youth worker, social responsibility officer) or as part of our congregational belonging, it's central to our understanding of what it means to live the Gospel. For some, the work for greater justice will be largely hidden, as in making the church community a more welcoming place. For others, as Maggie Butcher describes, a congregation may find itself part of some very public demonstrations of protest. Our concerns are not limited to the human community but, as Jennifer Wild suggests, we have a role 'in restoring and maintaining the flourishing of this planet on which we all live'.

Finally, alongside all our activities and explorations, prayer and public worship – particularly the Eucharist – feature centrally in most of the writings here. Amid all the ambivalence, the repeated exasperation with the church's attitude to sexuality, and the sheer sexism often encountered, there is still a sense that the Anglican Church gives each of us, in Janet Batsleer's words, 'a place and community of which I have over many years become able to use the word "we"'.

2.
'Another body on the bus'
Hannah Ward

It's not just that I'm a lay Christian, I think I'm probably a lay everything. I spent four years completing a professional training, to teach religious studies. I lasted two years. I loved my subject and (on a good day) enjoyed the young people I taught, but I just didn't have the going-out-to-work gene. The final straw was being ticked off by a deputy head for not wearing the right kind of shoes (my sandals were at the menders – I was wearing flip-flops, smart flip-flops). She suggested I was dressed for the beach ...

I didn't get to live by the beach – life has never put me there, alas. But I did the next best thing, perhaps, and (after a year's postgrad degree) joined a Franciscan community.

I had known the Franciscans well for about seven years, venturing to their convent in Somerset several times a year. It took most of those years finally to decide to give it a go. I had always felt strangely at home with Franciscans – as if they were my kind of people. As with others who have joined the Franciscans, there were one or two people I knew in other orders who tried to persuade me to join a 'proper' order instead. It made me more certain of my choice.

Living in a women's community as a novice also produced the raising of my feminist consciousness. I can even pinpoint the clanging sound of a dropping penny. It was a Thursday morning. Because none of us was ordained (this was about 1979/80), we had Father Monday, Father Tuesday … and Father Thursday, whose car broke down one day while we were sitting in chapel waiting for him. The sister in charge eventually appeared and announced that there would be no Eucharist that morning. No 'centre of our life' – as the Eucharist was described – because some bloke's car had broken down! I just couldn't understand why we didn't celebrate the Eucharist ourselves.

My time in the community was divided between the novice-training house in rural Somerset and two very different small houses in London: a house with much active engagement in Tower Hamlets, and a house in West London that reflected more than most the order's description of itself as a mixed active-contemplative order. It was living as part of the community in this last house that gave me real glimpses of how rich and diverse and impossible and fun and painful human life could be. I was going to say 'Christian life', but that feels too confining, not least because we weren't all Christians. There were two Franciscan brothers, a woman who was a Christian and an artist, and two or three young men who might otherwise have been homeless, who didn't tend to share our religion but did take their turn cooking.

As Franciscans in that house, we each worked part-time for some income, but we also encouraged the house to be used by groups who needed the kind of meeting space that could be provided by a large and comfortable living-room and small chapel (the rooms were combined for parties and other sorts of festivals). Regular users of the space were staff from a local campaigning hotel homelessness project, mothers of children with learning disabilities, members of the peace movement, groups from the

Movement for the Ordination of Women (MOW), and Women in Theology (WIT). The last of these reflected my own involvement in the Christian feminist movement.

It's not surprising, therefore, that after I left the Franciscans (via some months with the Community of St Clare, a contemplative community) Jennifer Wild (by then my partner) and I set up Womenspace, which was based at that same West London Franciscan house.

We had dreamed of setting up some kind of women's retreat centre but, with only a very temporary home and barely any income, that seemed more than a little way off. The resource we did have was the use of a comfortable meeting space with a large kitchen to make soup for those who might want to come straight from work.

We ran Womenspace for eighteen years (1989–2007), during which time about five hundred women came to one or more of its meetings. There was no fundraising, there were no staff, no one needed or received any kind of qualification; there was no booking, no deposits, no ongoing commitment for those who came. It was in every sense 'lay'.

We started Womenspace in 1989. The blurb on its programme describes it as 'offering women opportunities to gather around issues of religion and spirituality'. At the beginning, we gathered once a fortnight on a Friday evening for two hours. Some women came early – to share a simple meal, to have a post-work doze on a sofa, or catch up with whoever else might be there. We met at the Franciscan house in Paddington for five years, then for three years at a women's spirituality centre we had helped set up in Central London, and then, when that closed, for a year in the Rectory of St Martin-in-the-Fields. For the last year, Jennifer and I had moved out of London and after a year's commute on a Friday evening felt we couldn't continue in the same way. But by that time we were looking after the large garden at the Community of St Clare's guesthouse in Oxfordshire – the OP (Old Parsonage) – and had begun offering Womenspace weekends there two or three times a year. In addition, there were occasional 'study days'.

The format of Womenspace gatherings was always informal. The Friday evening meetings had a theme, which was introduced by someone, usually someone who had been to Womenspace before – we resourced each other. The same was true of women who led discussions on the weekends. We put details of evenings, weekends and study days on a simple leaflet, which we posted to those on our mailing list. We never advertised widely – word was passed on through Christian feminist networks and by word of mouth. There was no subscription, no membership. You took part by turning up – and there was no commitment to turn up again. Nobody 'joined' Womenspace. The Womenspace 'community' was the group present to one another on any one evening, day or weekend. Having said that, Womenspace did encourage and to some extent sustain a fairly large friendship network. Quite a lot of women who came to Womenspace made friendships that lasted well beyond the life of Womenspace itself.

The economics of Womenspace has puzzled some. We wanted no one to be prevented from coming for financial reasons, so there was a small suggested donation (£2 waged/£1 unwaged) for an evening meeting when we started. If you couldn't afford it, you didn't have to pay anything. If you could afford a bit more, that was very welcome. And that was how we ran all Womenspace events. In all the years we did so, we broke even. It was possible not least because of the attitudes and commitments of the Franciscan and Clare communities who offered us space. All who stay at the OP are asked for a donation rather than a fee. Those who came to Womenspace weekends had vastly different abilities to pay, but we always found that those who gave more made up for those who could afford either no payment or very little.

Womenspace hasn't been our only contact with the OP (convent guesthouse). Jennifer and I live in a neighbouring village and the convent chapel is our place of worship on a Sunday. Over the last twenty-five years or so we've also tried to look after the OP garden as much as we can (helped for quite a number of years by a friend who works miracles on the weeds that used to cause me to mow the gravel paths). Our familiarity with the house and garden made it easier to gather and host Womenspace and other groups there.

Womenspace was open to all women, however they described themselves in terms of religion or spirituality (we used both terms for reasons of inclusivity). Most of those who came were Christian, though a number were post-church. Others were post-Christian and a few practised religions/spiritualities other than Christianity. Others again worked for churches as ordained ministers, theological educators or in some other (semi-) professional capacity. We were always a very diverse group.

On three occasions, after the ordination of women in the C of E had happened, we asked ordained women to lead a discussion on an aspect of ministry/priesthood, hoping for some sort of dialogue between ordained and lay women. It didn't work. It was probably too soon (and I suspect still is) to hope that ordained women could begin to look at the meaning of priesthood (for example) with lay women. We could hardly believe our ears when we heard women we knew well say things like, 'It's a priest's (my) job to represent Christ to the people and the people to Christ.' On another occasion, an ordained priest from a church with a diverse congregation was left speechless when she asked those present to go round the room with each saying something about her religious/spiritual background. There's diversity and there's diversity! On each of the three occasions, it became clear that there was a real chasm between many lay and ordained women, which wasn't just about expectations.

I campaigned hard for women's ordination. Partly because I thought it was a justice issue, partly because I think an all-male clerical caste is a theological absurdity, and partly because I didn't think we could have some important conversations about the meaning of ordination and priesthood without women's full inclusion.

Now, with some urgency, I think we need to get on and have that conversation because many lay people (and doubtless some who are ordained) experience a growing and unhealthy clericalism, which has worsened since women's inclusion.

I'm not going to follow that train of thought because one major reason we started to gather the group out of which this book has come (the Lay Women's Group) was the tendency for all conversations about the church, or even Christianity more widely, to end up talking about ordination or the kind of church politics that really shouldn't sap the strength of most of us.

Having sketched out what some of living as a lay Anglican has been about, I want now to pull out a few threads of thought and see where they lead. They're about boundary, space/place, transition, friendship and not-knowing.

Bani Shorter, a well-known Jungian analyst, wrote:

To speak of borders is to speak of being contained and of moving on. For we reach a border by travelling from within; to be uprooted one must also have had roots; one is only aware of motion if one knows what it is to be still. Borders mark boundaries; they are thresholds. They signify the end of something old, the beginning of something new.[1]

[1] Bani Shorter, *Border People* (London: Guild of Pastoral Psychology, 1982).

Edgewise?

Many women who turned up at Womenspace were in some sort of transition – even if they didn't always realise it at the time. They may have been leaving marriages, wanting to change jobs, seriously questioning long-held faith, facing retirement or ill health. Some were exploring issues of sexual identity, others were surviving memories of sexual abuse. We recognised that for some 'regulars' to Womenspace there came a moment when we didn't see them again – their time of transition was over and they had either landed in new territory or stayed home but seeing it from a fresh perspective. We know this because women told us about the place of Womenspace in their times of change, often sometime later.

What had Womenspace got to offer women in transition?

Change doesn't happen overnight; the making of important decisions usually happens over time and involves the sense of a process. We leave one symbolic place and eventually, we hope, arrive at another (or return and know it for the first time). There's a beginning and an end, but the most important and difficult bit is the middle – or liminal – phase, the in-between, the neither here nor there and both here and there. It's full of dangers, lostness, struggle, potential, creativity and growth. It's a time of crisis – the Chinese symbol for which is formed by the pictographs for danger and opportunity. The liminal represents a gap that must be crossed, as in the Great Bardo (Bardo means 'gap') in the Tibetan Book of the Dead, that place between death and rebirth. Or the liminal is that time in a rite of initiation when the initiand is neither in their former state nor yet in their new state. The anthropologists Victor and Edith Turner have written about pilgrimage as a liminal (or liminoid, to use their term) phenomenon,[2] and Victor Turner has written about the

---

[2] Victor and Edith Turner, *Image and Pilgrimage in Christian Culture* (Oxford: Basil Blackwell, 1978).

early Franciscan movement as an attempt at 'institutionalised liminality'.[3]

When we're involved in significant life changes it's valuable to have the time and space to live the change without undue hurry or too much threat of falling apart. All kinds of things can help, depending on the nature of the decision or crisis: friends, medical professionals, financial support, the stories of those who have made similar changes, to name but a few. Womenspace offered a time and place to try out ideas, a chance to change your mind, hear yourself say something out loud that you didn't have to agree with the next time you said it. It offered some boundaries within which to do that – of time, physical space, a familiar pattern and some familiar people; the kinds of things that offer 'holding', which, in the title of our book, 'guard the chaos',[4] both in terms of protecting and valuing the chaos and taking seriously the need to guard against its negative drives. In this sense, Womenspace was a liminal space in which experiences of liminality could be held and explored.

A number of the women who came to Womenspace were, or had been, involved in Christian feminist networks, like Women in Theology (WIT) or Catholic Women's Network (CWN); others had long and actively campaigned for women's ordination in the Church of England and greater visibility for women more generally, in particular through inclusive liturgical language and expression. For much of the time I'm talking about, there was little feminist theology in the universities. Once feminist theology was taken into the academy and women were ordained and 'taken into the institution', the 'lay' Christian networks started to dwindle and the opportunities to explore feminist theology and liturgy

---

[3] Victor Turner, *The Ritual Process* (London: Penguin, 1969).
[4] Hannah Ward and Jennifer Wild, *Guard the Chaos: Finding Meaning in Change* (London: Darton, Longman and Todd, 1995).

narrowed considerably. The liminal space represented by those who had organised on the borders shrank markedly. Womenspace noticed this perhaps less than the networks, partly because we were small and not dependent on committee structures, but also because we weren't defined as 'Christian' (although Christianity was the religion that most of us belonged within or related to in some way, even if it was the one we had left) and because we weren't institutionally focused.

Networks like WIT and CWN created their own spaces in which all sorts of creative things could happen. There were opportunities for doing theology and meeting other Christian feminists (many of whom felt they didn't 'fit' in either church groups or secular feminist groups). These networks also provided opportunities for creative (I don't like the word 'experimental') liturgical events and new liturgical writing using inclusive language and a much wider than usual range of ways to talk about God/ess. Best known is Janet Morley's work, which was first published during this time.[5]

While opportunities for studying feminist theology continued in the universities, with occasional events open to women who were 'lay' theologians ('practitioners', as we came to be known) – most notably through the Britain and Ireland School of Feminist Theology (BISFT) – occasions to create and participate in feminist liturgy seemed almost to disappear. Although there are still local feminist liturgies, there is little evidence that the C of E feels it needs to take much notice of feminist liturgical work beyond finally recognising that 'men' really doesn't include women. God

---

[5] Janet Morley and Hannah Ward (eds), *Celebrating Women* was first published by Women in Theology and the Movement for the Ordination of Women in 1986 as a piece of 'barefoot publishing'. *Celebrating Women: The New Edition*, ed. Hannah Ward, Jennifer Wild and Janet Morley, was a greatly expanded edition, published by SPCK in 1995.

as She – in almost any form – is rarely allowed into public worship.

Liminal spaces are difficult for the churches. They are places of transition – in all directions. They are places where some people might find the freedom to acknowledge their need to belong to a church; they are also places where people can find the freedom to leave. Those invested in the institution as ordained or licensed ministers find that difficult. If you look at some of the churches' newer forms and projects that could potentially contain liminal characteristics (at least in terms of greater fluidity), they tend to be run or overseen by clergy, with jobs often open only to those who are ordained.

If we recognise that contemporary society is characterised by a good deal of change, which can lead to increasing stress and mental ill health, then perhaps the churches need to find ways of nurturing and developing liminal spaces. The most obvious of these are probably the retreat houses, a number of which in recent years have had to close for financial reasons. Few people can afford to go away for several nights (or even one night) – not just because of the cost, but also for reasons of time. We learnt from Womenspace that it's good to allow each other to drop in and out; that we have different patterns of commitment and belonging; that you can be truly committed to a group for two hours, without expectations that you'll see each other again. In all the years we ran Womenspace, there was never a gathering that didn't contain at least one person who had never been to Womenspace before.

Our cities, especially, need the sort of spaces where you can try out ideas, where you don't have to believe or do anything in particular, where you can discover who you are – contemplative spaces, if you like. These are not institutional spaces, even if institutions might offer the physical space. They are not places of 'ministry' either, but places of friendship. They are not about churchy words like 'pastoral care' or 'education', and certainly not 'teaching'. Liminal spaces are characterised by *communitas* – spontaneous, non-hierarchical community (hence the Turners' use of liminal/liminoid to describe early Franciscans and pilgrimage).

After we had run Womenspace for a number of years, we worked with a small Roman Catholic order of women to establish a women's spirituality centre in a building in central London. Although we achieved this, the project had only a three-year life and Jennifer and I experienced ourselves working there briefly as square pegs in round holes. It was partly that we didn't have the management skills necessary to run that sort of project (we major in gardening, cooking, and the making of coffee and friends), but significantly because we had always perceived ourselves involved in a peer self-help project with women who might use the centre, whereas the community of sisters saw it as part of their ministry. In the end, it wasn't possible for us to work together.

'Ministry' is problematic – more so when you stick 'lay' in front of it. Lay ministry is problematic because it so often refers to lay people being sucked into all sorts of churchy jobs and away from the places of encountering other human beings in their everyday lives. It makes almost everything need some sort of qualification (and control), from giving out hymn books and welcoming people, to visiting a member of the congregation who's sick and needs some shopping done. I'd like us to get away from the idea that everyone should have a ministry.

'I have called you friends,' said Jesus. I am suspicious of 'servant ministry'. Note, for example, how it's so often the vicar who washes feet on Maundy Thursday – supposedly as a way of 'serving', but in reality it comes across as just one more (rather good) opportunity for the vicar to play Jesus. (Often, I acknowledge, with the best intentions, but the symbol is easily corrupted.)

I spent long enough as a member of a Franciscan community (about nine years) to have been shaped by it in my understanding of the Christian way. Franciscans will have a go at almost anything – it's not a community for 'specialists', it's not very 'professional' (at least, it wasn't in my day), but it's quite good at accepting a mixed bunch, and Franciscans tend to be better at 'living it' than 'thinking it'.

At the heart of the 'living it' for Francis of Assisi was where he placed himself – outside the city, among the outsiders, encountering the travellers. It wasn't enough to nip out and preach a sermon every now and then; the outsiders weren't his congregation, they were his base. He might have horribly abused his body, but he knew it mattered where he put it. The title of this chapter comes from Malcolm Boyd, a US Episcopal priest active in the Civil Rights Movement (and later active in the movement against the Vietnam war and in gay rights). He wrote this about his decision to take part in a Freedom Ride in 1961:

> All the thought and moral processes that went into my boarding the freedom ride bus were not nearly so important as just being on it … Mine was another body on the bus. It didn't seem so important at that moment whose body it was. It was one of twenty-seven bodies pledged to be there.[6]

Malcolm Boyd put his body on the bus because he wanted to help bring about an end to segregation. Grace Jantzen comes at this 'living it' from another angle, but a no less physical one. In the

---

[6] Malcolm Boyd, *Malcolm Boyd's Book of Days* (London: Heinemann/SCM Press, 1968), p. 106.

Introduction to her revised edition of *Julian of Norwich: Mystic and Theologian*,[7] she reflects on what it might mean to be an anchoress in postmodern times. In the 'violence, greed and destructiveness, the cultural symbolic of the West', it is urgent, she argues, that there should be those who step back and 'devote themselves to thinking otherwise'. She writes:

> Part of what it means to be an anchoress in postmodernity must surely be voluntarily to enter a space – indeed, to become a space – where thinking otherwise can happen; where creative responses to the deathly structures of modernity can be discerned, that we in this new century may be 'endlessly born'.[8]

These words become even more powerful as I write them during the COVID-19 lockdown – a liminal space/time if ever there was one. Not only do one's immediate surroundings take on a new vividness (for good or ill), but it's a time also for revealing the starkness of the inequalities we live with – whether locally, nationally or globally. For all sorts of reasons, and for some people more than others, it's a dangerous time. But it could also be a time of opportunity – to see otherwise, to catch a glimpse of how much better and fairer and more compassionate our world could be. It's also a time when we've seen wonderful examples of *communitas* – whether virtual or in our neighbourhoods.

Throughout history and today there have been and are many different kinds of boundary-dwellers. To the monastics, anchorites and visionary protesters, we might add numerous individuals and small groups of people living in different ways at odds with the

---

[7] Grace Jantzen, *Julian of Norwich: Mystic and Theologian* (London: SPCK, 2000).
[8] Jantzen, *Julian of Norwich*, pp. xx–xxi.

cultural mainstream, many of them doing so as a way of living out and pointing to a more environmentally sustainable way of life. They are all a testament to the power of creating spaces and places where we can be held and supported to see and think the world (or a small part of it) differently.

This is an essentially lay task. I don't mean that ordained or other professional people can't do it – though they have to leave an awful lot behind (careers, for example). But the creation of these liminal spaces requires a kind of boundary living that is hard if not impossible for the people whose concern it is to maintain those very boundaries. They are also spaces where 'not-knowing' is vital – it's what gives life to the search for something bigger, something more beautiful, more just, more human and more divine. The church is frightened of not-knowing, despite its apophatic tradition.

Buildings and community seem to play an important part in helping to make the kinds of creative spaces I've been talking about. For us at Womenspace, we were dependent in large measure on Franciscan and Clare communities who generously shared their resources and kept out of the way. When we were suddenly without somewhere to meet in London, St Martin-in-the-Fields did the same. Buildings and gardens are a wonderful resource. They can provide both a sense of spaciousness and a firm sense of containing boundary, things necessary for exploration in times of transition. And a sense of community, a community of friends, no matter how temporary, provides another sense of containment, as well as joint endeavour and companionship.

So why does it rarely feel as if churches provide these kinds of spaces?

Their boundaries aren't porous enough, and leadership styles undermine community (at least of the spontaneous *communitas* sort) – it's difficult to build a sense of peer community when everything has to go through the vicar. Our chaos needs a bit more space, our not-knowing a lot more encouragement, and our commitment to belonging celebrated in the present and not demanded in the future. At Womenspace, Jennifer and I were the only people expected to be there next time there was a gathering.

And there are two of us – companions on the Way, and civil partners. According to the comments of some who came to Womenspace, the fact that it had this relational quality mattered. I think it did to some, and not to others, but neither of us would have ever started Womenspace alone. I find the C of E's position on 'issues of human sexuality' so ridiculous that I can't really engage with it at all (though I have to when meeting with hurt human beings), but I am aware and grateful that as a lay woman I have nothing to lose by living as myself and so much to celebrate in partnership.

'I'll be there.' Those were the words that first came to mind when I started to think about this chapter, to think about what it means to be a lay woman in the church. I'm not altogether sure why, but they probably reflect how important I think the physical, the material, the bodily is to whatever the Christian life is about. Incarnation, in other words. Where we put ourselves matters. How we relate to our environment matters. What we make of the challenge to call each other friends matters. My faith, if you like, has been more about where I've put myself, and with whom, than what I've believed or, at times, even desired. For whatever reason, I have been and still am a boundary-dweller; there are professionals who dwell on boundaries, often at great cost, but it's more naturally the place of the lay person.

3.
Extracts from the diary of a lockdown

Margaret Beetham

26 February 2020

Lent begins today, Ash Wednesday. Since I was not brought up to the ritual of the solemn Eucharist, I always find astonishing and strange this ash on the forehead, the words reminding us of our mortality.

When you are old, as I am, the command to 'remember you are dust and to dust you will return', which the ash of this Wednesday signifies, is powerful indeed. I know I must be near the end of my life. I have scattered the ash of my dear dead ones. Ash is unruly. It flies about in the wind. Dust and ashes!

In my childhood in India, devout Hindus would apply the traditional three stripes of ash to their foreheads in honour of Lord Shiva. These were just part of my world, as inexplicable as that some men wore dhotis and some trousers. Or the presence of the holy men around the great Temple to Meenakshi in the city centre, their bodies splashed with red and white, colours whose meaning, I now know, is as complex as the many faces of the gods; fire and ash; life and death; male and female. I was not puzzled by these as a child nor by the ubiquitous presence of red

33

and white stripes on roadside trees or temple walls. What felt strange was their complete absence in Britain.

Ash, like water, carries some basic meaning for us humans, which surfaces in different ways in different religious traditions. Ash from the burned tree carries a double meaning of the destructive power of fire but also the power of the tree, the cross in Christian thought, to renew itself and grow. On my morning walk today I passed the huge stump of the old ash tree in the local park, from which now a forest of upright twigs has sprung, pushing their black buds into the air.

As I walked through the park, I realised more fully this moment, now, this Lent; the lengthening day, the snowdrops fully out in the garden, the daffodil buds showing yellow. Everything is early this year. Everything is greening and growing.

29 February: Leap day

Who can I propose to? What can I propose on this extra day, this extra-ordinary day?

I am thinking about being 'of dust', being ordinary, everyday, and specifically about being 'lay'. To be lay is to be, as the online free dictionary tells me, one of 'the hoi polloi, mass, masses, multitude, *people*, the great unwashed, the common *people* generally'.

'Hoi polloi' was one of those expressions I loved but didn't quite understand as a child. Now I am old I see that one doesn't want to be one of that lot after all. Who wants to identify as being among the great unwashed nowadays?

'Lay' is a word used mainly in the context of the church, and the church in its official pronouncements always says lay people are important. 'We are all lay,' they say, but these pronouncements tend to be made by those who are ordained and by definition not lay. To be called 'lay' means that you are not 'of the priesthood', not ordained to special function. You are an everyday sort of person. The word lay still carries these connotations of disdain or even disgust that the online dictionary suggests. How to be the hoi polloi of the church, I wonder.

What today can we propose for the place of the laity on this extra day of grace?

Saturday, 7 March

Today I and my friend Janet joined hundreds of other women on a 'Walk for Women' in central Manchester. It was a fine spring day. Together we took up the width of the busy shopping street and stopped the traffic. 'Just like the 70s,' someone said to me. Well, it was and it wasn't. Yes, we had our bands and our banners. We felt connected to each other. But, also, wonderfully, this Walk was not all white women. There were black, brown and white women all walking together. Janet and I walked with the Chinese Women's Group. We wanted to be in solidarity with them as the Chinese community is being blamed, even physically attacked, for the coronavirus that is spreading round the world from China. Behind us was the Women's Institute banner. The WI! Never seen on a 70s' march to my knowledge. And, the banner they carried was decorated in the colours of the trans movement, or so my friend told me. Who knew? So, not like the 70s!

And, it was billed as a 'walk' not a 'march'. A march is purposeful. We marched in the 70s to make demands: for nurseries, equal pay, access to contraception. A walk does not demand. It is an end in itself. The difference only became clear to me when we reached our destination, St Peter's Square, the pedestrianised space in front of Manchester Library, called after a long-demolished church. We milled around. Someone had laid flowers at the newly erected statue of Emmeline

Pankhurst that lurks behind the tram stop. Unlike the city fathers, who stand twice life-size on top of huge stone slabs around the corner in Albert Square, Emmeline is a diminutive figure. She looks as if she has just scrambled on to an old kitchen chair to be heard above the din, her arm stretched out in mute appeal.

I expected at least a rousing speech, a bit of 'What do we want?' 'Equal pay!' 'When do we want it?' 'Now!' rhetoric but here was none. We were told again and again by the organisers that we were wonderful. Women were wonderful. Today was wonderful. And please go into the library for interactive projects. This was not a march but a walk.

So; it was not 'just like the 70s'. Then, we shared a project – to change the world. We did not tell each other we were wonderful. Perhaps we should have done. We were in too much of a hurry. We demanded that inequality be addressed. 'Sisterhood is powerful,' we said, and it was. Collectively we made change happen, but there was not always happy agreement between the sisters and the sistas and the sistahs and the sistren.[1] 'We have come a long way,' one friend texted me after the Walk , 'but still a long way to go.' 'Amen' to that. What do we want?

I was never among those who in answer to that question shouted, 'The Ordination of Women'. I could not understand why women wanted to be part of an institution I saw as unreformed, male-dominated, irrelevant. Of course, women should be able to be ordained if they had the necessary skills and a desire to be so. But, for me, that was not where the battles were. It was the ordinary of women's lives we wanted to address: childcare, the place of domestic labour, including care of the sick and elderly;

---

[1] See Bernardine Evaristo's dedication to her wonderful novel, *Girl, Woman, Other* (London: Penguin, 2019).

low pay; harassment at work; domestic violence; the right to love another woman. These problems of the hoi polloi.

Sunday, 8 March: International Women's Day

I went to church this morning and was delighted to find that we had an all-women team; even the two acolytes (it is that kind of church) were women – Julia and another lass whose name evades me, both asylum seekers. Afterwards I said 'Well done' to Richard, our rector (non-stipendiary and on a 0.5 post). He looked puzzled. 'All-women team on International Women's Day,' I said, but he laughed, said it wasn't planned. It just happened. Is that good? Women are there now in those roles. They don't need to be specially trundled in for the odd 'women's' occasion.

We were told not to give each other the Peace with a handshake because of the coronavirus, which is spreading into Europe now, so we waved or bowed and smiled. Taking my example from four young nurses sitting behind me who, I know, come from Kerala, I offered the Indian *namaste*, hands pressed together. We are a mixed bag, the ordinary people of the Church of England in this year of grace 2020.

Tuesday, 10 March

Today I went to see a friend. I shall call her Jane. I have not seen her for what feels like a long time because she has been ill and was not up to meeting in our usual local cafe or, indeed, meeting at all. I drove to her flat and we sat at each end of the settee in her lovely light room. We have been told that we need to keep two metres apart because of this virus and we were probably nearer than two metres but still not close. She is a priest, a remarkable woman whose wisdom I cherish, as I do her – I think 'kindness' is the word, though it has become worn a bit smooth by careless usage. She is kind, she recognises we are all kin, all of humankind.

I knew something of her history as she knew something of mine, but today for some reason, perhaps because she was still frail or because we were not in the noisy cafe, she began to tell me the story of the last twenty years of her life as a priest in the church. At one point she stopped and laughed and said, 'This is becoming a confessional, you know, but it is I who am doing the confessing.' 'I will treat everything you say as confidential,' I said.

After an hour and a half or so she was exhausted. I so much wanted to give her a hug but we have been told we mustn't, and she has been ill, so we waved our hugs to each other. I drove off in such a rage at what I had heard that I nearly crashed the car. I had to pull in to park in a suburban street so that I could calm down. Her story of abuse, of – to put it kindly – lack of care for her shown by those who should have looked after her, had shocked me. 'They are all too busy trying to protect their backs against charges of historic child abuse to pay attention to what is going on now,' she said. When I got home, I felt like sitting down to write angry letters to various senior church figures, but instead I went and stomped around the local park.

The women who had campaigned for women to be ordained did not just want to add a few women like Jane into the mix. They wanted a different kind of church. And the ordination of women has achieved much. Last week, Cherry Vann, who has been for a long time in this diocese of Manchester, was consecrated Bishop of Monmouth in the Church in Wales. A woman bishop is not so remarkable now as it was a year or two ago. There are a few, but Cherry had made clear to the appointing committee, and makes public now, that she and her civil partner, another woman, will occupy the Bishop's House together. 'You must listen again on *Woman's Hour* to her interview,' a non-churchgoing friend texted me. 'It was great.'

Yes, but the C of E has just brought out a hugely damaging

statement about human sexuality, which says, 'No sex except between a man and woman married to each other.' I was so angry that I made a formal proposal at the Parochial Church Council that we write a collective letter of protest, but by the time I had drafted it the Church Fathers had scrambled back, saying, 'Oh dear! So sorry! We shouldn't have pressed "Send". We will let you know in a few months what we really think. Lots of love from the C of E.'

'When will they ever learn?' as we sang in the 1980s.

We have achieved much, we much-derided feminists: two women prime ministers, equal pay legislation, the fact that I can now rent a television without having to get my husband's written permission. But, the list makes me want to laugh and cry at once. Equal pay! Ha! Not just at an individual level but whole sectors defined as 'women's work' are grossly underpaid – like care. Hospitals are now sending very sick people into care homes to clear wards for coronavirus patients. Immigrant men, too, of course, take up these jobs – feminised jobs, 'low skilled' jobs, so defined by people who wouldn't last a week working in a care home.

So it wasn't just about getting a few women priested. Jane's experience showed that.

As I walked round the park past the daffodils and under the trees with their just thickening buds, trying to deal with my rage and my sorrow for my friend, I remembered an essay written by the American theologian Beverley Harrison, back in the 1980s or maybe even the 1970s, 'The place of anger in the work of love'. When I got home, I rang a friend I thought might have a copy. 'I will look on my shelves,' she said. She rang me back a few minutes later. 'Yes, I have an ancient collection falling to bits but it has the essay in it. I am self-isolating but if you can get yourself here, I will put it on my doorstep and you can pick it up.'

Beverley Harrison's argument is that neither quietism nor turning our back on the world to create women-only safe spaces will do. Anger at injustice is a necessary part of the work of love. The church has counted anger, or 'wrath', among the seven deadly sins, but this ancient tradition, she argues, misreads both the Jewish tradition of prophetic denunciation of injustice and the gospel stories of Jesus' anger at, for example, the money-changers in the Temple. It was not the 'Gentle Jesus, meek and mild' I learned about as a child who went into the most sacred building in Judaism and threw things about, upsetting the financial and religious hierarchies both literally and metaphorically.

Drawing on the liberation theology of the South American churches, Harrison argues that it is with those at the bottom of society who understand the need for justice and, therefore, the need for anger at injustice, that the church will be renewed. She wants a church of the ordinary, the multitude, a word much used in the gospel stories for the earliest followers of Jesus. Multitude, the great unwashed, the ordinary people.[2]

'We are gentle angry women', we sang at Greenham Common, but holding these qualities together is not easy and I am not sure we did it. I have not written those letters. Perhaps I should.

Wednesday, 11 March

More news of the spread of coronavirus and the government is saying people should stay at home, especially the old and vulnerable. That's me.

---

[2] Beverley Wildung Harrison, 'The Power of Anger in the Work of Love: Christian Ethics for Women and Other Strangers' in C. S. Robb and Beverley Wildung Harrison (eds), *Making the Connections: Essays in Feminist Social Ethics* (Boston, MA: Beacon Press, 1985), pp. 3–21.

Extracts from the diary of a lockdown

In the Co-op I was served by a young West Indian heritage woman who I know is doing a nursing course but comes back regularly to work behind the till. She helped pack my shopping, then leaned across the counter and said, 'Now, go home, love, and wash your hands. We all have to look after each other now.' I smiled all the way home at this exchange with a young woman who in another life might have been my granddaughter.

Looking after each other. Isn't that what ordinary people do? Women, especially, have had the task of looking after children, the elderly, those who are less able. In churches that still have anyone under 50 in their congregation, women continue – as they have for generations – to be Sunday school teachers. But, more regularly, their task has been to be on the flower rota and to make the coffee after the service. In the church I attend, the flowers are arranged by a middle-aged man who is a secret artist and who ran a florist shop for many years. His flower arrangements are hymns to beauty. They 'praise God in the sanctuary', as the psalmist said in quite another context. So, we don't have a 'flower rota for the ladies'.

Those other homely ministries, those of the coffee cup, the biscuit plate, the home-made cake (there are lots of Cake Sundays in our church!), these are also important. Asking someone 'How are things?' as you pour them a coffee can lead to a brief but important exchange. It can be a way of looking after each other. However, it is still strongly gendered. A crucial moment in the early days of the women's liberation movement of the 1970s was when women in radical and left-wing circles began to refuse their male companions' regular, 'Make the coffee, love, will you?' (implied, 'while we go on with our important discussions'). Eventually, we turned. 'Make your own, mate,' we said. 'Oh! And I'd like one, too. Thanks.'

Not so in the church, where still on the average Sunday it

will be women filling the coffee cups and washing them up or loading the dishwasher. I do it myself. So, is that the task of the laity, the ordinary people, or at least the ordinary women?

Thursday, 12 March

I went to early morning yoga. Only three other people there in what is usually a class of twenty. Back home, both my daughters rang me, obviously a pre-planned double attack, telling me that I must 'self-isolate'. Horrid term. The coronavirus is spreading. I promised them I would think about it and, yes, I would be careful, but then I went out this afternoon and met a younger academic colleague, now a friend, in the local coffee shop. He was in Manchester for a check-up at Christie's Hospital round the corner. He has been diagnosed with a rare cancer. He is obviously not 'old' but he is 'vulnerable'. Should we be in the Costa at all? What were we going to do with this new virus spreading across the world? What will happen to his cancer treatment?

Friday, 13 March

Various friends are 'self-isolating'. My inbox is full of messages asking how I am, telling me to stay at home. My neighbour offers to do my shopping. The sun is shining and I and my friend walk to the river through the Mersey Country Park. We keep a little distance apart if not quite the regulation two metres. The hawthorn is greening. Creation renews.

Among the branches and broken twigs brought down by the storms of February, celandine shine out, small yellow flowers opening in the sun. Celandine always seem to me the hoi polloi of spring flowers, close to the ground, small and unshowy. Once established, it is very difficult to get rid of, as gardeners know.

Everyone of my generation knows that Wordsworth wrote a poem about daffodils. Only nerds like me know that he wrote two to the celandine – not his best verse perhaps, but still … I decide to reread Wordsworth during this time of self-isolation. He would have called it 'solitude', which could bring its own 'bliss'.

After a lot of hesitation, I decide not to go to Chorus rehearsal this evening. There are a lot of us, all very close together, and apparently singing really does spread the germs around – just like sneezing or coughing. I miss the singing. We are rehearsing Benjamin Britten's *War Requiem*. I love this music, the interweaving of Wilfred Owen's poems with the words of the Latin requiem, the passionate desire of the composer for 'wars to cease'.

People are already beginning to invoke the great British myth of THE WAR in relation to this virus, but it will be very different and not only because it seems to be lethal for the old rather than the young. 'Keep calm and carry on.' The slogan of 1939 has been recycled recently, encouraging us all to accept the war on the poor that government austerity has inflicted. It makes us acquiesce in the growing inequality, the stripping down of those public services that are particularly important for the vulnerable, the old, the mentally and physically frail. Now the cost is becoming clear. Keeping calm and carrying on, just being in our own little bubble, won't do now. Everything will have to change after this virus has run its course. Perhaps our motto should be 'Do Not Carry on Carrying on'.

Today a video is going round showing Italians living in the isolation of extreme lockdown, but they are singing to each other across the street. 'It made me cry,' one person wrote online. Me, too.

Whatever happens I hope we can go on singing together. Church is one of the few places other than football matches where people sing together, even if they 'can't sing'. At one point in church I regularly sat just in front of a woman with a glorious soprano voice and, next to her, another who sang loudly all on one note. Sometimes it really annoyed me but mostly it didn't matter. We all sang the Gloria happily together. Our small choir in church is mostly women – another lay ministry?

Saturday, 14 March

A Quiet Day in church which means that after morning Eucharist the church is open all day for people to be in silence. Some come for the whole day, some for an hour or two. They/we meditate, pray, go to sleep, read a book or just sit in the sort of suspended consciousness that sitting in silence in a space like this can bring. Traditionally it is what old women do. Certainly, when I was younger I felt I had no time in my life for this kind of silence, or perhaps I did not make it. I wonder if now I can keep the silence for other people – my busy colleagues, my neighbours, perhaps for the community. I am agnostic on this as on so much else to do with 'church'. I know that this keeping of silence is important in many traditions. A Buddhist friend has come here, and my Quaker friends know what I am talking about.

St James's Piccadilly in the heart of London's West End is open for silent prayer every day and pews are set aside for the homeless to come in and sleep safely during the day. Here the homeless who come are likely to be members of the congregation, asylum seekers or refugees. Julia, the young woman who carried the big candle last Sunday, comes and sits for a long time.

Julia comes from Uzbekistan. Her father and brother have told her in graphic detail how they will kill her if she goes back. She cries silently at the back of the church. Then she gets up and scrubs down all the surfaces in the kitchen, puts the clean cups out for tomorrow's coffee. She has just been given the right to remain in Britain. Just in time, because coronavirus will close the courts where appeals are heard. However, Julia now does not know where she will live. She must leave her current room in a shared house in Rochdale and hope that her benefits can be sorted out and she can find a place to live. How will she and others like her manage now with this new virus spreading? I want to give her a hug, but I can't.

Sunday, 15 March

All sorts of confusion about the virus on the news. The only solid advice is to wash your hands. Mine are already sore from washing. Apparently, if enough people get the virus (and presumably die off), there will be a magic thing called 'herd immunity'. I have accepted somewhat gracelessly that I won't go on public transport or go into public places. However, I am going to church where special precautions have been put into place. 'Be Anglican,' the churchwarden says. 'Sit as far apart from each other as you can.' Everyone was directed through to the back to wash their hands as they came in. Specially wiped hymn books. No wine at the communion. No tea or coffee. Some stayed away but I wanted to come. It is the anniversary of my sister's death tomorrow and she is remembered in the prayers here, as she is every year. It is important for me that she is remembered by name. 'Let light perpetual shine upon her,' everyone says. I don't. I am trying not to cry. Dust to dust. Ashes to ashes.

When I get home, my inbox is full. The telephone does not stop ringing. Everything is being cancelled. We scramble to set up alternatives to our book group on Tuesday, but what about the fun meal five or six of us had set up for Friday? Messages fly around. I am in the house on my own but not alone.

Monday to Wednesday, 16–18 March

A mad three days. Thank God for email and Zoom (which I have learned to use this week) and Skype and all the other ways we keep in touch. The weather has been glorious, so every day I have had a local walk, usually in the woods and wetlands of the Mersey Country Park, sometimes with my friend Janet. The hawthorn is greening.

Among the exchanges online are messages from the women in our Lay Women's Group who are scattered all round the country: London, Exeter (Uganda), Northumberland, Birmingham, Yorkshire, Manchester ... This is not the place to rehearse how I found myself going back to the church, an institution that I had quit years before in rage and disgust. Perhaps it is enough to say that it was partly connected to the death of my sister and partly that I did not go back into an institution. I joined a group of people who shared something, something I began to explore and to want to share with them.

Nearly twenty years ago now, when a crisis in my life led me to need time out for a while, I took a friend's advice and went to stay in the guest house of a Franciscan community in Oxfordshire. It was a retreat house, but there were no rules other than that you respect others in the house and turn up for meals (cooked by someone else). If you wanted to be in silence, you could take meals in your room. If you wanted to talk, the other guests were at the table. We were a mixed lot. You could attend any of the five daily services but you didn't have to. The chapel was open from 7.00 a.m. to 9.00 p.m., usually with only the cat lying on the floor (there was underfloor heating) or a member of the Community sitting, presumably praying and meditating, or sometimes snoring gently in a corner. You paid what you could afford.

This was how I became a member of the 'Lay Women's Group' brought together by Hannah and Jennifer, two remarkable women who were Franciscans, had been members of the Community but now lived close by, still keeping their links to the Community and doing the huge guest house garden. They still do the garden and are still the people I ring, as I did today, when I need some wise advice or just to have a natter. We can't drink a glass of wine together as we usually do when we meet but we can talk on the phone.

They got together the 'Lay Women's Group'. We are mostly retired now, with one or two exceptions. Most of them worked in church ministries in one way or another: as industrial chaplain, educator, academic theologian, leader of church organisation, back-room staff to a senior churchman. Most were involved in the campaign for the ordination of women, though clear that they themselves did not seek ordination. I was none of these, and listened when they talked about how women no longer have access to the kinds of posts they had held, partly because they are no longer being funded as the C of E shrinks, partly because women who are deeply engaged in the life of the church assume that the only legitimate 'calling', to use the ecclesiastical term, is ordination.

My experience of being in church more recently was different but connected. I call it 'badging', the obsession with ensuring anyone who undertakes any role in the church, however informal, has to have a 'badge' from some clergy-run course. There are some formal roles, such as 'Reader' where women (and men) not ordained can perform certain public roles in worship when this seems wise, but, while some clergy are very happy to think that lay people might have skills and knowledge to contribute, others are not. Clericalism rules. Not OK.

Thursday, 19 March

I slept badly and felt low when I woke today, Thursday, as the implications of what is going on sank in. First thing, I dropped my old Pyrex measuring jug on to the stone floor of my kitchen where it shattered into pieces. I burst into tears. It's only an old jug but I have had it for more than fifty years and used it constantly. How stupid to cry over that! Then I got a text. My next-door neighbour. 'I just heard a crash in the kitchen. Are you OK (*worried face*)?'

I rang her back and felt much better. Her younger daughter has been sent home from school with a cough but now all the other children will be at home, too. Her husband is the head of a big secondary school in a deprived area of Manchester. They will have many children to look after, of both front-line workers and those in vulnerable situations. I fear that the stigma of being declared 'vulnerable' may be so powerful that some refuse to accept it, just as some children refused free school dinners because they were stigmatised. 'I am alive now because of free school dinners,' one of my dear friends said. 'School dinners saved my life.' And now? I sweep up the Pyrex pieces.

Through the door comes a message. Some of the people in the street have divided the street and taken ten houses each. 'Here are our names and phone numbers,' the note read. 'If you need shopping or prescriptions collected or want to ring for anything, here is the name of the person and the number for your group of houses.'

Friday, 20 March 20

A friend emails to say she is reading Defoe's *Journal of the Plague Year*. Of course, terrible epidemics have long been part of our history. The Black Death, the waves of cholera up until quite recent history, and, in the 1940s, my brother in India and my brother-in-law in Devon both had polio – 'infantile paralysis', it was called then. They nearly died and many children did, a worldwide epidemic. But now, with vaccines and good health care, we think it's all past history. Or that it only happens in other countries. Places like China, or 'Africa', that great continent whose very different nations get lumped together in the British imagination. But here? We conveniently forget the AIDS epidemic because it only affected those 'other' people, not us, nice heterosexual British folk. But now? Perhaps I should read Defoe or Camus' book on the plague, *La Peste*.

I remember Thomas Carlyle's *Past and Present*, his bitter attack on the inequalities of nineteenth-century British capitalism. I find my battered old hardback, bought in a second-hand bookshop when I was a student. Carlyle became more and more authoritarian and even racist in his later writings. Here in this early work he advocated the monastery as the ideal community, a paternalistic solution, perhaps, but still his analysis was sharp.

I have a bookmark in the place I want, Carlyle's account of an earlier epidemic, the dreaded cholera, and of 'the Irish widow', a member of a despised immigrant community, who in her destitution went round the various 'charitable institutions of the City', set up by rich capitalists to dispense charity to 'the deserving poor'. All denied her, 'she sank down in typhus fever; died and infected her Lane so that seventeen other people died of fever in consequence'. Carlyle points out that it would in the end have been an 'Economy' to give her support. The action of those who think all that matters is 'the economy' is in the end self-defeating.

I read on ...

The forlorn Irish widow applies to her fellow creatures, as if saying, 'I am your sister, bone of your bone; one God made us ...' They answer, 'No, it is impossible; thou art no sister of ours.' Until she proves her sisterhood; her typhus fever kills them; they were brothers, though denying it! Had human creature ever to go lower for proof?[3]

22 March: Mothering Sunday, Mother's Day

In the church's calendar this is Refreshment Sunday. Halfway through Lent, some of the Lent discipline is suspended. It is a day for celebration. The sun is shining. Daffodils are out. A blackbird sings in the garden.

As Carlyle knew, capitalism is a greedy beast and has tried to transform Mothering Sunday into a business opportunity for florists, card-makers and those who run restaurants, but it has not succeeded in remaking this day in its own image.

Traditionally this was called Mothering Sunday because it was the one day in the year when working people were allowed the day off to go home. Those who had moved away not only from their mothers but also from their communities and from their 'mother' church, the church where they had been baptised, returned for a few hours today. In nineteenth-century Britain hundreds of young girls who worked as domestic servants could today see their mothers. I think of them, girls younger than my granddaughter, walking or getting lifts in carts – and how much they must have tried to pack into this one day.

How long till I can see my daughters? How long till I can hug my grandchildren?

Today across the country families are Skyping and ringing each other up and feeling sad because they can't be together or feeling that more intense sorrow that comes from mourning those they have lost. Children mourning parents; parents mourning children who have died or those who have never been born.

---

[3] Thomas Carlyle, *Past and Present* (London: Chapman and Hall, 1893), p. 128.

Extracts from the diary of a lockdown

The church has long been in a mess over mothers. In the Protestant tradition where I was brought up, Mariology equalled idolatry and a severe masculinism prevailed. But even in churches where we name the Mother of God regularly we are in a muddle about motherhood. Is it what women ought to do? Shall we punish those who do not or cannot bear children and punish those who do by making them carry the burden of caring? And what of the image of 'Mother Church'? Is being 'lay' simply to recognise my brothers and sisters?

Today all church buildings are closed. I light a candle and join in listening to the live-streamed service from our church. It is not like being there but it does connect us as a worshipping community – at least those of us who have the resources to do so.

I have a Zoom meeting with the friends who were due to come to mine for Sunday lunch today. We can't eat together but we can talk and share our stories. We come from very different places and different communities of race and culture but we have stopped noticing that. We were brought together some years ago around the campaign in church to support one of us from being deported back to Rwanda, where her family had all been killed. She is now a dear friend, much loved and valued by all of us and by the community of those diagnosed as HIV positive and their families, whom she supports.

Yes. This will be a very different Lent from any we have experienced before. Many of us will be alone through the days of Maundy Thursday, Good Friday and Easter Saturday to Easter Sunday. But, of course, we are not alone. We are connected, not just by technological wizardry but by being church. That is who we are, we lay people.

I put my laptop and a bunch of daffodils on the table, a gift from the friend who has been doing my shopping. I sit down to wait for the message inviting me into our conversation.

4.
In darkness and obscurity
Helen Stanton

Like many women, feminist or not, the ordination of women to
the priesthood in the Church of England was a watershed in my
life. Had I been a man, I would have offered for priesthood as soon
as I could after university, but instead I took a number of contracts
that enabled me to exercise a kind of ministry. I do not think I
was waiting for change, just getting on with what seemed to have
meaning at each step of the way. By the time women's ordination
to the diaconate and to priesthood became possible, I knew being
a parish priest was not for me, though I longed to be able to fulfil
a sacramental role, and still do. Women's ordination continues
to be important to me, and is the main reason – sometimes the
only reason – I have for not becoming Roman Catholic, where
my commitment to the Eucharist as absolutely central to the
Christian faith is honoured, in a way I see diminishing in many
parts of the Church of England.

The (to me) recent story of women's ordination in the
C of E was part of my radicalisation, which began in a theological
and spiritual conversion in the 1970s to the political left through
the influences of Methodist and Anglican students at the Queen's

Foundation for Ecumenical Education, at which I now teach. Socialism is not the kingdom of God, but many of its values are congruent with God's reign.

After my first degree I spent two years working for a local ecumenical project in Sheffield during the miners' strike, when my core feminist principles began to find articulation. It was, however, when I was working as a researcher at what is now the University of Derby that I had a major crisis. At the end of the General Synod debate on Women's Ordination in 1978, Una Kroll shouted from the public gallery, 'We asked for bread and you gave us a stone.' I was doubly shocked: at the result of the debate (to delay further action on this subject) but almost more so at Una's words. This strange response caused me to examine myself again. Was conventional politeness really more important than justice? Did protocol take precedence over prophecy? It took me some time, but this too was a kind of conversion, a *conversio morum.* My encounters with children with mental health issues and my exposure to life among impoverished people in Central America reinforced a liberationist stance that remains with me, though my activism is less public than it once was.

In the years approaching the legislation to allow women to be ordained as priests in the Church of England, I campaigned with the Movement for the Ordination of Women and promoted feminist theology through Women in Theology and other groups. I learned about beautiful alternative ways of conducting meetings, sat on pavements in support of nuclear disarmament and joined in celebrating Mass at Upper Heyford.

Shortly before the passing of the women priests Measure, I was a university chaplain in Sheffield. It seems miraculous now, but we ecumenical chaplains gained episcopal permission to celebrate the Eucharist in the same room, with a common ministry of the word. For the most part the presiders at the Eucharist were an Anglican priest or a Free Church ordained minister, with me supporting. The other table was presided at by a Catholic priest. What was noticeable, however, was that when no ordained person was available for the Free Church and Anglican table, only I, with my licence from the bishop, was able to administer communion from the reserved sacrament. When a Catholic priest was unavailable, a number of catholic students might administer. This was familiar to me from El Salvador too, where lay Catechists would lead the ministry of the word – except for the absolution – even when priests were present. There was a sense in which the Catholics trusted lay people more than Anglicans did, and in which Catholic bishops were willing to allow local priests to authorise lay people to do so, without hierarchical involvement. It has become noticeable to me since women's ordination, and not necessarily related to it, that needing a licence has become more prevalent in the life of lay people in the C of E.

The day a two-thirds majority of each of the Houses of General Synod agreed that women should be priested, 11 November 1992, was one of the happiest days of my life. I was at Church House, Westminster, with dear friends, and went back to Sheffield full of energy, buoyed by the applause with which my two deacon friends were greeted as we entered the train for our journey. The ordinations in 1994 were glorious occasions, joy palpable and infectious.

A few months after these ordinations, I met a newly priested friend for coffee, and heard her say, 'All the women in the diocese have been invited to Church House on a particular date. I wondered if you were coming too?' I was a university chaplain at that time, and was often treated as an honorary cleric. No, I wasn't invited, and did not feel excluded. But, 'all the women in the diocese'? How would they fit into the new Church House in Rotherham, even all the church women? Perhaps this was a foretaste of the future. Was it George Bernard Shaw who said, 'The professions are a conspiracy against the laity?'[1] I have never been sceptical about 'expertise', and, while recognising since my first encounters with socialism and feminism that no scholarship (or any thinking) was without its own vested interests or ideology, 'professional advice' or scholarly research was something I respected, especially when it acknowledged its own shortcomings. Here, however, in a Sheffield cafe, there seemed to be a sense almost of a cabal. Were the women I lived among at the university – the students, the cleaners, the academics, the researchers and administrators – not only not clergy but now somehow not women? I am sure my newly priested friend did not mean any of this, but I noted it with suspicion as well as humour.

Now, I must make it clear that I believe in ordination; I believe in its sacramental nature. I am one who is sometimes described as having a 'high' view of priesthood. But is any lay calling inferior to that of ordained people? Just as women and black people (and I could name many other groups) need to hold 'closed' gatherings to share their particular concerns and, in solidarity, to develop particular strategies, so I have no difficulty recognising the need for 'closed' clergy meetings and concerns. I certainly did not mind, in 1994, the women priests of the diocese meeting together without male priests or lay people.

I do wonder, however, if the existence of women priests might have reinforced clericalism as a 'conspiracy against the

---

[1] And coming from Bernard Shaw's *Man and Superman* (anti-) hero, Jack Tanner, given to prolonged and hyperbolic rhetoric, it is unclear to me what Bernard Shaw meant by this.

laity'. Many ordained people, men as well as women, strongly resist this, but institutionally I wonder if the phrase 'going into the church' for those in the C of E does not still mean ordination rather than discipleship? When women could not be ordained, it was very difficult to argue that priesthood was inclusive and representative. Somehow, afterwards, there was an opportunity to pretend it was, despite the tiny numbers of black and Asian priests, difficulties for LGBTQI+ communities, and a certain resistance to working-class people, typified by the Green Report.[2] Ministry, in common parlance, has always seemed to mean 'ordained' ministry, even among those who take a less 'high' view of ordination than my own.

Melvyn Matthews, a senior clergyman whom I number among my friends, while Chancellor of Wells, often spoke of Laity A and Laity B. Laity A were those who helped run the church, while Laity B exercised their ministry beyond the church and supported by it. I guess my own vocation has been on the edges of Laity A, in that while I have had a preaching ministry, I have never, since I was an undergraduate, had any desire to help run a parish. On the whole, though, I feel most sad that Laity B seem to receive less of the church's support, encouragement and resourcing than Laity A. It seems to me that Laity B are the frontline disciples, though Laity A deserve our honour and respect too.

Being a church professional while a lay woman was fascinating. I was especially honoured and encouraged during my time as a social responsibility officer to have the support of my bishops, and to have the delight of working with people who on the whole saw theologies of the reign of God, of social justice and social action as at least one way of being a disciple.

---

[2] The strangely named *Talent Management for Future Leaders and Leadership Development for Bishops and Deans: A New Approach* (2014).

I learned a lot, not least about farming and creation care. I had the privilege of representing 'the churches' on probation and social service committees of the county of Somerset, and of laughing about my official role, because so many of the other members of such committees were also Christian disciples. I was able to support some of the work of the Children's Society with Travellers at that time also.

Primarily – thank you, Bath and Wells – I was able to interpret my role as a theological one. My commitment was to the idea that the whole people of God were theologians, and I followed my academic supervisor, Professor Elaine Graham, in regarding reflection upon the *practices* of churches as key to theology, and of vital importance to the development of theological understanding wherever it occurred. My conviction, shared by many others in the diocese, that social justice was key to the Gospel, meant the focus of my work was on 'mainstreaming' social responsibility. If social transformation was at the heart of the good news, that meant – and means – prioritising the marginalised and poor, those who are oppressed and neglected.

In very little of this was my lay status called into question, though I was frequently asked why I was not ordained, since I was clearly some kind of church 'leader'. (There were a few years in which I felt anyone who showed any kind of leadership – of whatever sort – was pursued for ordination.) I still wonder, however, whether the acceptance of my lay status did not at least partially derive from the fact that 'social responsibility' was seen as not necessarily at the heart of the church. Not like liturgy, for example, though I want to affirm with Stanley Hauerwas that 'liturgy *is* social action'.[3] This is partially why I want to

---

[3] S. Hauerwas, 'The Gesture of a Truthful Story', *Theology Today* 42:2 (1985), pp. 181–5.

encourage my priestly brothers and sisters to go on presiding at the Eucharist even without a congregation in this time of the Covid-19 pandemic, for is not the transforming of the world, as well as those who call themselves 'the body of Christ', distilled and made real in the celebration of the Eucharist?

The inspiration of liberation theologians, of feminists and of adult education models meant that hearing the voices of lay people, and of those even more absent from the churches, directed at least some of my work. I had good lay and clergy supporters in this, and I had learned from my beloved friend and colleague at Christian Aid, Bridget Rees, how to speak up, how to 'interrupt' the more powerful who often saw the status quo as neutral, rather than quite as ideologically ridden as movements for change. I sought to encourage the examination of our taken-for-granted thinking.

I had been energised by working on *Something to Celebrate*[4] around the diocese and enjoyed greatly working with people of diverse views on *Issues in Human Sexuality*,[5] and on racial justice. I loved working with the Jerusalem Trust on family support work. I had found it a privilege to spend time with pressurised clergy who sought support from me, which they sometimes felt they could not seek from other clergy because of a culture of competition. Walter Wink's analysis[6] of the church as an institution that was overcome sometimes by the principalities and powers began to resonate more strongly with me, as I saw people – and not at all just in the diocese where I worked – bullied and sidelined. Sometimes the hierarchy of the church seemed to be responsible

---

[4] *Something to Celebrate: Valuing Families in Church and Society* (London: Church House Publishing, 1997).
[5] *Issues in Human Sexuality: A Statement by the House of Bishops* (London: Church House Publishing, 1991).
[6] Walter Wink, *Naming the Powers* (1984), *Unmasking the Powers* (1986), *Engaging the Powers* (1992), all Philadelphia, PA: Fortress Press.

for this 'abuse' of power, and sometimes lay people, who, having held positions of power outside of the church, exercised that power inappropriately within it. But, as Wink argues, sometimes no one is directly responsible; it is just that, however good our intentions, institutions as well as individuals are sometimes overcome by evil.

So why, sometime after I left Bath and Wells, did I move into the training of clergy? In part because theological education had been the heart of my social responsibility work. In part because I had been involved in training clergy alongside my social responsibility job, and I loved it. Education as formation, it seems to me, is key to discipleship development, and clergy are always disciples. Training people for ordained ministry also seemed a way of promoting the liberation theology I so loved among people of influence in the churches. Whatever else clergy are, they are gatekeepers, and I wanted to encourage the pushing open of the gate to all, especially to those whom Jesus called 'poor'. Andrea Russell's recent poem says this more eloquently than I can:

> Outside the walls
> beyond the moat
> by the Penniless Porch
> I met an angel,
> juggling.[7]

As someone committed to Laity B, I nonetheless moved nearer and nearer not only to Laity A, but Clergy A. I hoped and hope to be part of a learning together, and I feel very privileged to work now somewhere that is in tune with liberationist

---

[7] Unpublished. Reproduced by permission of the author.

theologies. Queen's is a place that tries to prioritise the vulnerable, that seeks to include 'minorities' in its learning and teaching, which, though far from perfect, sometimes mirrors something of God's reign. I learned, however, that the closer I came to the 'centre' of the church, the more tired I became. On the whole I worked and work with others who share many of my commitments, and who challenge me into some deep questioning of them. Yet it feels that the church has become more hierarchical since women have been ordained. I see with deep sadness responses to the pressures of the times that seem less and less 'of the Gospel'. I see fire in the ashes of decline, but an unwillingness to recognise and wait for the work of the Holy Spirit in that decline, and a throwing on to the ashes of what seems like some inappropriate fuel to create a superficial, if sometimes spectacular, blaze. I wonder what I am sending out our ordinands and student ministers to face? And I fear the evidence that, despite our attempts to the contrary, some former students, and their peers, still talk and write of long-term congregants as 'not proper Christians', or nominal believers, while maintaining an 'us' and 'them' in the church, which is surely a travesty of the body of Christ.

Most significantly, I wonder what I am doing in training priests as I witness an apparent, and not universal, decline of the Eucharist as the central act of worship in the Church of England. Priests are vital to the Eucharist: they preside, lay people celebrate. And, in spite of what I have said about solitary presidency, I believe this is where discipleship is most fully resourced and our Christian identity formed.[8] As we all – lay and ordained – offer up ourselves and the world to God whose love is unbounded and

---

[8] I assert this while at the same time honouring intentionally non-eucharistic churches, like the Salvation Army and the Quakers, who often so palpably embody the body of Christ.

eternal, we offer all life for God's transformation. We celebrate the embodiment of God in the world, in the poor, the oppressed and the neglected, in beauty and compassion and friendship. We offer ourselves, that more and more we may embody – by God's grace – the way of the incarnation. And in all this, I believe lay people share in priesthood, the priesthood of the one who came to us, that we might return to God the Blessed Trinity. The Eucharist is not only a distillation of this, but is also the locus – spreading outwards further and further – of God's real and loving presence. To quote one of Janet Morley's beautiful, and unauthorised, Eucharistic Prayers:

> In the body broken and the blood poured out,
> we restore to memory and hope
> the broken and unremembered victims
> of tyranny and sin;
> and we long for the bread of tomorrow
> and the wine of the age to come.[9]

As I have indicated, on coming nearer and nearer the 'core' of the church I have become more tired, and in some ways more disillusioned. I have less energy left for national work. God is gracious and calls to me in darkness and obscurity. As the church seems to resist the darkness of God's presence, of uncertainty, even death, I want to embrace obscurity, powerlessness, defeat – though I also resent them all. At least partially, I appreciate the diminishment I experience or imagine, and that sometimes brings me near to a new creativity of which Sister Anke[10] and

---

[9] 'Eucharistic Prayer for Good Friday' in Janet Morley, *All Desires Known* (London: SPCK, 1992), p. 53. Reproduced by permission.
[10] Sister Anke, *The Creativity of Diminishment* (Oxford: Fairacres Publications 109, 1989).

Joan Chittister write. And though I do not now know a life in ruins, and as a white, western, middle-class woman can scarcely claim ever to have done so, I am struck by Sister Frances Teresa's comment that we never really learn to pray until our life is in ruins.[11]

I wonder whether the apparent fear of so many church leaders and congregants about falling numbers, and a question about how many will return to public worship as that becomes more possible, is not a failing to embrace the liminality of which Hannah Ward speaks in an earlier chapter of this book. That all life is in a time of transition in places of war, environmental degradation, political turmoil and COVID-19 is unavoidable. What more can we do than offer the life of the world to God, do what we can, and, to quote Dietrich Bonhoeffer in another time of turmoil, 'throw ourselves upon the mercy of God'. Many people believe they live best with certainty, with the strong sunshine of clarity and surety. But are not, to quote Morley's take on Psalm 139, 'the darkness and the light ... both alike to [God]'?[12] And the darkness of uncertainty is where we live now, and may be where we have always lived. Yet, except for the mystical tradition,[13] too often the church has thought of darkness as something to be avoided, even feared. Yet, 'There is in God, some say, a deep but dazzling darkness':[14] not knowing is part of what it is to be human. And God does not leave us alone in the darkness. Darkness is where we face the sorrows of the world, the

---

[11] Frances Teresa OSC, *Living the Incarnation* (London: Darton, Longman and Todd, 1993).

[12] 'For the Darkness of Waiting', in Morley, *All Desires Known*, p. 58.

[13] Represented by many men and women, including the priestly author of *The Cloud of Unknowing*, but perhaps most unhierarchically by Teresa of Ávila, a Reformation mystic, in her late work *The Interior Castle*.

[14] Henry Vaughan, 'The Night'.

frustrating lack of understanding, and the enticing mystery of life, in which God may meet us and renew us.

If churches, at least in the North and West, are in decline, so in those same places is religious life. Yet it seems to me that some religious offer an unassailable insight into decline. Are religious sisters and brothers lay or ordained? In the Lutheran and Anglican churches, most men religious, and some women, are ordained to the priesthood. Profession is certainly not entirely unlike ordination, but usually nowadays without the pomp. The church does not name profession as a sacrament, however, though abbot (and abbess?) were regarded as fathers (mothers?) in God. As I come towards the end of this chapter, I want to use some resources from religious to point to ways in which, by the grace of God, lay people might regain their key roles in incarnational and eucharistic living at this time of darkness and obscurity.

Joan Chittister, in the book to which I have alluded throughout this essay, *The Fire in these Ashes*,[15] uses the extended metaphor for the decline of traditional religious life, of the burying of the embers of a fire at the end of the day, so that they may live, unseen and unfelt, until the fire is lit again and they then ignite the fire more swiftly and generously.

Religious life can be a – sometimes eccentric – paradigm of Christian discipleship, and yet I wonder whether being a religious sister or a friar might not be a useful paradigm for discipleship. It might just enable a vision where clergy are important but not superior, and where the church is not dominated by clericalism but by a vision of the whole people of God as missionaries and ministers in their own callings, each with their own authority,

---

[15] Joan Chittister OSB, *The Fire in these Ashes: A Spirituality of Contemporary Religious Life* (Leominster: Gracewing, 2001).

appropriately celebrated by the church. Hannah Ward somewhat mischievously, but seriously, wonders whether all Christians should be ordained. The Methodist Church of South Korea emphasises this in its Ordination Service by noting most of the functions we associate with ordination as belonging to all who are baptised. And perhaps too this is what lies behind William Countryman's thinking:

> By 'priest' I mean any person who lives in the dangerous exhilarating, life-giving borderlands of human existence, where the everyday experience of life opens up to reveal glimpses of the HOLY – and not only lives there but comes to the aid of others who are living there.[16]

For Countryman, everyone is in some sense a priest, just as everyone bears God's image.

Perhaps being lay women in a clerical church enables us to be pioneers of this way of thinking and being. And there are signs of this. In some places I see lay women licensed (though I am not sure bishops always realise the implications of what they are doing) to lead communities in formation, exploring, sometimes centimetre by centimetre, what it might mean to be church, the body of Christ, in areas dominated by those who approach the divine very differently; learning to be presence, and a prophetic voice, while seemingly on the margins. And I see among those whom I have taught, clergy who have been called into what I might call Clergy B. I especially think of a wonderful woman whose ordained ministry, alongside the lay ministry of those who live in her parish, has its centre in a cafe on a white working-class

---

[16] L. William Countryman: *Living on the Border of the Holy: Renewing the Priesthood of All* (Harrisburg, PA: Morehouse Publishing, 1999), p. xi.

housing estate. When last Easter, after celebrating the Eucharist in the parish church, Catherine celebrated with those at the cafe – serving behind the counter, pouring out coffee, offering pastries and Easter eggs – I wonder: is this not a sharing in the life of Christ? A sharing distilled in the offering of the Eucharist?

These examples give me hope that another world, and indeed church, may be possible. But as Countryman and Chittister suggest, this is a risky business: it means living courageously as church, priests and people, and perhaps especially as bishops. The world as we know it may be coming to an end, and I think we are called to live with that, and in it, not rush forward to solutions that make us comfortable. Waiting with our hands lifted to God, literally and metaphorically, is all that we can do, and all that we are required to do. Participation in that priestly offering is for all people, and is to enter into the life of God.

One of the beloved bishops with whom I worked once said that he saw the decline of clergy vocations as the cause of the decline of the church. Despite my belief in the significance of priesthood, I rather doubt that. As Chittister writes of declining religious life, 'To live until we die may, in the final analysis, be the ultimate goal in life.'[17] And we can all – lay or ordained – allow God to help us do that.

---

[17] Chittister OSB, *The Fire in these Ashes*, p. 60.

5.
A lay industrial chaplain on Tyneside, 1977–90

Caroline Barker Bennett

I arrived in Newcastle upon Tyne from Surrey in the summer of 1977. I bought a house for £6,000 in a terraced street in Heaton grandly named 'Fifth Avenue'. 'The Avenues' were originally built at the end of the nineteenth century for railway workers. There were large sidings on the main Edinburgh–London line close by, and in the early days the 'knocker up' would come round to bang on the windows to rouse the drivers and crew for early shifts.

Fifth Avenue had a back lane for access but at the front the street was grass with a central path. It had been a prototype for the upgrading of terraced housing to avoid demolition. Residents had agreed to give up their front gardens to make the grassed play space. In 1977, the houses were still mostly Tyneside flats: upper and lower flats with two front doors side by side. Many were owned by the City Council and used for housing the elderly. A few were privately owned and some had been converted into houses. On the corner of the street was a bakery and shop where two of my neighbours worked behind the counter.

In the South I had worked as a teacher and youth worker.

I had spent six years as a youth worker, first in a youth centre attached to the Church of the Holy Spirit, Clapham, and then in an ecumenical youth project in the southern part of Southwark Diocese. During that time, I 'read theology' with Cecilia Goodenough, who had just retired as Assistant Canon Missioner in Southwark. I then completed training as a Lay Reader in 1976. I had also been part of the Southwark Pastoral Care and Counselling Scheme. It was the time of Southbank theology: the South London Industrial Mission and the then Canon Missioner, Ivor Smith-Cameron, offered courses and projects to link the inner and outer parts of the diocese – 'Faith at Both Ends of the Commuter Line', as it was described. All this had helped me to grow as a person and to develop pastoral and group-work skills. Ordination was not a possibility. Would I have offered myself if it had been? Wishing to move on from youth work, I applied for a variety of jobs unsuccessfully. In several cases I was interviewed and felt that, as the only lay, female candidate, I was there to confirm to the panel that they needed a clergyman.

One day I was talking on the phone with Peter Selby, who had recently gone to be Canon Missioner in Newcastle Diocese. He said, 'Have you ever thought of being an industrial chaplain? We need one in this diocese.' I hadn't ever thought of it but decided to apply, while Peter discovered whether the Church Commissioners would agree to pay me. The interviews were about to happen, but by the time they did I was the only candidate. The interview took place in a steel stockholding company in Sunderland. As I waited to see if I was to be appointed, I saw a photograph on the wall of a woman who had taken over the firm in the 1860s after her husband had died. I felt it might be a good omen! It was. I became an industrial chaplain for Newcastle Diocese in the ecumenical Northumbrian Industrial Mission team of eight full-time chaplains and some part-time chaplains, all clergymen, covering north Durham, Tyneside and parts of Northumberland. We had chaplains in the coal industry, at the steel works in Consett, at Reyrolle Parsons and Clarke Chapman engineering works, Swan Hunter shipbuilding on the Tyne and a chaplain in Sunderland. This list now reads as a memorial of great names in the industries of the North East which were to decline or close in the thirteen years I worked on Tyneside. One chaplain was exploring links with small businesses.

Training in industrial mission

I began, in the autumn of 1977, with a period of training. There were several memorable experiences. I visited Consett with the chaplain and talked to a woman operating the huge machine that rolled out the sheets of molten steel in the rolling mill. She had worked at the job during the Second World War but was stood down at the end of it so a man could take it on. She had found other work, but after the Sex Discrimination Act 1975 she had come back. The Works were to close in 1980. I spent time with an official of the Transport and General Workers' Union, who took me with him to see the excavation work on the Kielder dam then being constructed to provide a huge reservoir of water to supply the steel industry on Teesside – another industry that was to contract in a few years' time. We went to find the shop steward who had the membership record and subscriptions. We traced him to a rural caravan park, where the trail went cold. I felt I was seeing the very outer reaches of the great Union's work! I also went to a meeting of the Tunnel Liners' section of the Union. They were building the Tyneside Metro and the Union official was anxious that they had good safety equipment. The men, however, preferred better wages, which recognised the dangers of the work, to better safety precautions. I was embarrassed because, when we arrived, the meeting was told that a lady was present and they should mind their language! I spent a week with ACAS and sat in on an industrial tribunal and went to Reyrolles to attend the chaplain's lunchtime discussion group of management and shop-floor workers. Such groups were held to be the heart of industrial mission activity and promoted communication between different levels of big companies. I talked to a man working in the stores, who had worked for many years at Rolls Royce and could remember all the part numbers from his time there: now redundant knowledge. It seemed a parable about skills that were being lost.

The main part of my training was to spend a month at the Wills tobacco factory, a distinguished art-deco building, opened on the Coast Road in 1950. My time was billed as 'work experience' but I was not allowed to do any 'work' and instead spent my time in different departments talking with the people as they worked. I started in 'the splitters', where cigarettes that had been returned from retailers were opened up and the tobacco salvaged for recycling. The floor had to be swept with care so no trace of tobacco was lost. When the excise men visited, the residue was weighed for refunding. At the time, the working day in most of the factory was quite relaxed, with frequent tea breaks available to the workers in the 'tea bays' in the wide corridors of this state-of-the-art factory. There was also an excellent canteen where the supervisors had their breaks and everyone went for lunch, apart from those who were served in the management dining room. I had been apprehensive about how I might be received with my posh accent and double-barrelled name. I remember being quizzed by one of the supervisors: if I 'belonged Surrey' why did I want to move to Newcastle? It seemed that my accent was perceived as being southern more than posh.

It was a very exhausting month because, except when I went to the loo, I was engaged with people in conversation, often conducted against the noise of machinery as I tried to master the Geordie accents. Those I met were welcoming, and as yet the shadow of closure, which was to come in 1986, had not loomed. By the end of the month I felt I had experienced everything from being a 'new starter' to release into retirement!

Chaplaincy in engineering

The engineering works where I was to be chaplain was George Angus Fluid Seal Division, a factory on the Coast Road at Wallsend. The oil seals made there had many applications, from the motor industry to aircraft and medical equipment. It had been a traditional family firm – if work was short, workers were taken to the owner's farm in Northumberland to work there, returning with gifts of vegetables. By the time I went there it had been bought by a multinational company. My predecessor as chaplain had visited for a number of years but had then got involved with a broadcasting project, which was expected to take a few weeks but which took over his time. He had not gone back to the factory to say goodbye. Three years elapsed before I was appointed.

This meant that when I arrived I faced questions about what I was doing and what I hoped to achieve. No doubt these were always questions that chaplains in industry were asked, but here they were more pointed. As I visited for the first time, people said, 'Yes, we used to enjoy seeing your predecessors when they came round for a chat. But we never quite saw what they came for. They did organise discussions. We quite enjoyed them at the time, but looking back it's difficult to see what they achieved or were really meant to achieve. Then they seemed to stop coming. Now you've started. So what are *you* hoping to achieve?'

In a sense, I never entirely answered that question. Industrial mission was never about trying to recruit church members but it was about helping the church to be aware of industrial developments and the realities of people's working lives while supporting those who worked in the particular workplaces where we visited. I always felt daunted on the days when I was to visit. As I drove there I used to commit myself in prayer to what the day might bring: what the Quakers call 'centring down'.

Once there, I would try to work round different departments, but it was easier to talk to those in the labs or those who worked manually without machinery than, for example, in the press shop where men ran up and down tending their bank of noisy presses, with few possibilities for conversation. Although I found it hard, I was aware after a time that I would be sorry to be told that I was not going back. Perhaps because they were at work and under time pressure, people tended to talk about things that were important to them, that they were angry about or that were worrying them, more readily than they might have in social conversation in the 'outside world'. I felt I was being received with warmth in a place where life was very much going on.

My closest relationships tended to be with the women who worked on the shop floor. Two, who were shop stewards, have remained friends after thirty years. When I started I was afraid that being single and with no children would mean that my experience of life would have few connections with the women workers I met. But I soon found that the stuff of everyday living was shared.

Did the fact that I was a woman and not ordained make a difference? Initially my lack of clergy status probably made people unsure about my role, possibly thinking that they had been sent 'second best'. But at the time there were no women deacons, no women in dog collars. Tyneside having a strong

Roman Catholic culture I felt made people see me as some sort of religious. Being female and lay also had some advantages. As a detached youth worker, I was used to infiltrating myself into groups. This was an important part of the role and could be done more easily without a dog collar. After a time, I used to meet with some of the women outside work. It began with meetings in the Newcastle Labour Club, where they insisted on buying me pints to their halves! Very soon, however, we started meeting in our houses where tea and cake were more on the menu. This felt much more natural for us as a group of women.

How was I seen by the men? It was not made explicit, but I sensed that some felt it was all right for a woman to be spending her time going round talking to people and finding out how they were, but hadn't a man better things to do with his time?

I started visiting in the spring of 1978. The first redundancies were announced that autumn, and as time went on this process gathered pace until people were going every month and the feeling in the factory became, 'the sooner this place closes and we are all made redundant the better'. People felt this despite knowing that for many of them getting another job would be impossible. In 1978 there were some 1,800 employees. Twelve years later there were about 550. My chaplaincy, like those of my colleagues, became a ministry to industrial decline.

The clothing co-operative

I had been under pressure from my colleagues to take on more factory visiting but was reluctant because I did not want to visit another large works. I had enough challenge in making sense of George Angus!

In 1981, the local news was full of some women who had staged a sit-in in their clothing factory in South Tyneside.

With support from Tyne & Wear Council and the North East Co-operative Development Association (NECDA), they set up as a clothing co-operative, Louise Argyle. I managed to meet the women at the 'Back to Jarrow March', marking the seventy-fifth anniversary of the original march and protesting about current unemployment rates. I asked if I could come to visit them, and after the first visit managed to keep going back. I was prepared to help in whatever way was needed. Sitting and cutting off loose ends of cotton with one of the workers was a good way of learning about the organisation and getting to know the women. At the beginning they had orders for children's clothes, but these did not last. The difficulty was that while there was work everyone worked on the machines, completing the order, but scouting round for other work was difficult. A manager was sent by the NECDA to help, but his relationship with the co-op members was problematical. His role was advisory but tipped over into management, which they resented. It may have been he who secured an order from Barbour's to make up jackets. He left as this work was starting. It proved to be the lifeline for the co-op, which became, in effect, an outworking department of that company. It was a relationship that lasted for several years.

Relationships were often turbulent. The members were wary of anyone who appeared to be becoming bossy while at the same time knowing that there needed to be planning and that disputes needed to be resolved. Often when there was a row someone would leave. When I came to record conversations with the members in 1983–84, their views of the co-op were diverse.

June, one of the founding members, said, 'We've had to learn the hard way. We've had a lot of strife, lot of heartache, lot of upset. But at the end of the day – and we're still learning and we've still a long way to go – but my opinion about the co-op – it's the best thing that anybody could do. For all the ups and downs it's better working for yourselves than working for someone else.'

Pam, who came to work as a trainee, said, 'I mean, it's not right. They should have a boss in here, definitely.'

Julie, who joined after the beginning but brought much useful experience including managing in a bar, said:

> When I first started at Louise Argyle I was just dismayed. I just couldn't make head nor tail of the place. I used to think, 'My God, I've never worked in a place like this before in my life.' I mean, you had the boss and the workers – not everybody was the boss! You didn't know who to speak to. I was just bewildered.

Nevertheless, she stayed.

Alice, a founding member, said, 'I wouldn't start another one and yet I think the time will come when all these big factories will close down and it'll all be co-ops . . . Everybody sort of managing their own – I think it's a good idea really.'

I enjoyed my relationship with Louise Argyle. It was good to see how the women who had experience of managing a home and much experience of working as machinists in clothing factories adapted to managing a business: to negotiating with bank managers, grant-giving organisations, and so on. During my time there, two of the founding members died: Betty, with whom I had sat and talked on my first visit, and Alice, who had become a friend and who died a drawn-out death from cancer. I was able to take part in their funerals and speak of their experience at work and their contributions to the co-op. Being able to bring the working life experience into what is said at funerals is a valuable contribution that industrial chaplains can make.

The developing network of women chaplains

Soon after I started in the all-clergy team of eight chaplains in the Northumbrian Industrial Mission, lay women were appointed in other areas, thanks to an initiative by the Girls Friendly Society (GFS): Alison Norris in South London Industrial Mission, Anne Borrowdale in Teesside, and others. The GFS was founded in 1875 to support working girls living away from home. The appointment of women industrial chaplains in the 1980s brought a focus on women workers to industrial mission and a feminist challenge to its teams. By the 1980 Industrial Mission Association (IMA) Conference there was a small number of women chaplains. We set up what was initially a support group but became the IMA Women's & Men's Network. I benefited greatly from having this support and stimulation. The Network was partially responsible for encouraging the Church of England Industrial Committee to produce the report, *And All that is Unseen: A New Look at Women and Work*, written by Rosemary Dawson with the help of a working group of Alison Norris, the Revd Chris Beales and myself.[1]

Researching women workers

At this time I began to feel the need to 'do something' with the experience I was having. I had learned a great deal about factory life and especially about the lives of the women I met. I undertook an MA with the Department of Sociology and Social

---

[1] Rosemary Dawson, *And All that is Unseen: A New Look at Women and Work* (London: Church House Publishing, 1986).

Policy at Durham University and wrote a thesis: 'Speaking as We Find: The Experience of Women Workers in Tyneside Industry'. I recorded conversations with nineteen women I knew through my work. I asked them about their working lives: what they did when they left school and how they had moved from job to job. The eldest had started work in 1934 and the youngest in 1981. In the first place I was struck by the vividness of the reminiscences and moved by the hardships that many of them had endured and often taken for granted. I became aware that what was emerging from the conversations was a history of working-class women's employment on Tyneside in the period covered. The jobs open to women were limited and the women I interviewed had done most of them. Shop work was considered socially preferable to being a 'factory girl' but in practice they were dependent on relationships with those in charge; they had no trade union protection and wages were less than factory wages. The clothing industry was a staple employer of women but, as we have heard, it was subject to sudden closures. Most of the women I interviewed had left school and started work between 1945 and 1975. Jobs were easy to come by in those years. It was only the older women, who had left school in the 1930s, who were haunted by the spectre of unemployment, as were the very youngest, looking for jobs in the early 1980s and being employed on the Youth Opportunities Programme.

In the 1930s, domestic service was always an option for women. It was avoided by all but one of the women I talked with, but as Vera, born in North Shields in 1921, said about jobs available to her when she left school in 1935:

In those days the only thing that there was in this town was either the Fish Quay, 'the smoke house' as we called it, Hutton Haggies (the Rope Works), which was out, and Tyne

Brand. I had no fancy for Tyne Brand – or service … so it was the Fish Quay [where her mother worked]. I left school on the Friday at 4 p.m. and I got started the Saturday morning on the Fish Quay.

Well, then, I started at 14 as what they called a 'twopence halfpenny learner'. Now that was, you got twopence halfpenny an hour for your work. Now you only worked when the work was there. You weren't on a set wage. You only got paid by the hour, so it meant 'No work, no money'. Sevenpence an hour was the highest wage you could achieve.

Vera went on to describe how hard the life was:

There was an awful lot of hardship to the point where women were pregnant, married women. Now I've worked in a yard where a woman was standing working. She's taken her labour, the boss has had to put her on the lorry, take her home. Within a few hours that woman has had her baby. Within a few hours, we'll say a day, that woman has been back working because times were such in those days – no work, no money. The baby was brought to work with her in the pram and it used to be a communal pram. The one pram used to be passed from one, you know, if somebody was pregnant: 'Keep on to your pram!' And the pram was brought and, mind, if you had a good boss he would let the pram stand in the office to keep the baby reasonably warm. And the mother, when the baby needed feeding, she used to have to go and wash her hands, remove her oilskins, sit and feed her baby and there it went on.

Because she wasn't fit for military service, Vera worked in a munitions factory in Scotland during the war. After the war, her working life reflected both the ups and downs of industry on Tyneside; developments in working conditions for factory workers and employment-related legislation. When she returned, she said: 'I wasn't so keen to go back on the Fish Quay after having been in a factory and found that working from 7.30 in the morning to 5.30 at night, that was your day over.' She worked in engineering works on a new industrial estate. When the company she worked for retreated to its headquarters in Coventry, she reported, 'We were the very first factory to be made redundant with payment.' Government policy was encouraging the development of light engineering in the North East, in part to replace job losses in heavy engineering and in part to provide jobs for women. Vera got a job with Ronson's, who were building a factory in Cramlington to make hair-dryers – an example of the rising demand for consumer goods. She started at a local unit and was made a supervisor. When the time came to move to Cramlington, the firm wished Vera to be a supervisor with a training role. She was offered a house in the new town. Her husband worked in the Wallsend shipyard: 'It's one thing me moving house for me husband's benefit. But, I says, "No way, if he can keep his job in that shipyard, he's going to keep it, and no way would he travel." So of course I had to turn it down.'

Despite being upset by this, Vera, who had no children, thought that at 48 she would enjoy more freedom and opportunity to do more for her mother. But she soon found she missed work and got a job at George Angus, which was where I met her. Having worked full-time for some while, she found her mother needed more looking after and arranged to go part-time. Her neighbour looked after her mother in the mornings and Vera split her wages with her. After her mother died, Vera went back to full-time work until she retired on Job Release aged 59. In retirement she helped to look after her neighbour's little girl and they went on day trips by bus.

I have told Vera's story at length because it encapsulates so much of what I heard from the women I interviewed for my research, with its interweaving of personal experience and family pressures against the background of Tyneside employment history.

Industry and education links

As jobs for school leavers became more and more scarce in the 1980s, teachers were at a loss about how to prepare students for life after school. 'Should we prepare them for unemployment and a life of leisure?' was the question. I had a friend, the head of a community high school on a large housing estate, who was concerned to address the question. He engaged the Bishop of Newcastle and the Diocesan Board of Education in the issue. The challenge was to respond, on the one hand, to the disappearance of traditional jobs, including apprenticeships, and on the other, to 'the new technology' – computing and electronics. I got involved because of my contacts in industry and training, and we convened a group in 1982, with representatives from industry, the careers service, different sectors of education and training to explore the issues.

At first there was suspicion from industry: the young people they met could not add up or spell and were lacking the discipline that working life required. On the school side, the feeling was that industry only wanted robots. After trust grew, what emerged was that in order to fit into the work scene young people needed to be flexible and able to work in groups: no longer would they find that the jobs they went into would last their working lives. The group (Tyneside Education and Employment Group – TEEG) discussed various challenges: the nature of the school curriculum and examination system; the tradition in the North East of young people leaving school as soon as they could; the lack of suitable training schemes with funding available to the young people who took them up. These were all issues that concerned the Thatcher government. The Bishop was able to draw together senior figures from the region for a conference in 1987. The group meanwhile had organised smaller conferences, and visits and events, aimed at bringing together people from the different sectors involved and helping them to have an understanding of what innovative projects schools were undertaking and what was happening in local industry. We were much helped by the involvement of a manager from British Telecom. He had been a member of the TEEG from the beginning, and in 1989 he was seconded to work with local education and business partnerships. Business in the Community, one of the Prince of Wales' charities, also started in the North East, and in partnership with them we worked to replicate The East London Compact.[2] The idea was to set up a contract between schools and local businesses: relationships would be developed and targets for students agreed with a view to school-leavers being guaranteed a start in a job or training.

I had been elected to the General Synod in 1980 on a ticket of support for the ordination of women. I was the only industrial chaplain on the Synod and was able to speak on employment-related issues. I was also appointed to the Board for Social

---

[2] The East London Compact, launched in 1987, was modelled on the Boston Compact. This inspired the Thatcher government as a means of improving attendance and raising attainment in inner-city schools. In 1988 Norman Fowler, Secretary of State for Employment, launched a £12 million National Compact Initiative to promote Compacts in other British cities. See William Richardson, 'Education–Business Compacts', David Finegold and Laurel McFarland (eds), *Something Borrowed, Something Blue? Part 2: A Study of the Thatcher Government's Appropriation of American Education and Training Policy*, Oxford Studies in Comparative Education 3:1 (Oxford: Symposium Books, 1993).

Responsibility and its Industrial Committee. I went as a member of the Committee's delegation to lobby Lord Young at the Department of Trade and Industry. We were there to voice the church's concern about rising levels of unemployment. It gave me an opportunity to mention the work we were doing about education and employment in the North East, which strengthened our links with government departments in the region.

In 1990 I felt the time had come to move on, and was appointed Diocesan Director of Education in Manchester. I was very sad to leave Tyneside and have kept my friendships there and my affection for the region.

Reflection

Looking back on my life in Newcastle thirty years after I moved on I realise that it describes a particular era. The Church of England has moved away from what might be called frontier ministry in favour of more traditional concepts of mission and evangelism. Industrial mission is out of fashion. The employment patterns of the North East have changed greatly and many of the jobs that the women I knew were doing do not exist today.

After working in Manchester and Bristol dioceses as Director of Education, I have finally retired to the Wylye Valley in Wiltshire where I share a miller's house beside the river with my sister. We have created a large vegetable garden in what was just a field and have chickens, ducks, geese, three dogs and a cat. I sing in a church choir, which visits the ten churches in the benefice on a rota. The services I attend are very traditional. The team rector is a young woman. She has a male house-for-duty colleague and there is a team of non-stipendiary priests: one man and three women and a woman Reader. So the years when we battled for the ordination of women have borne fruit. But it is very different from the inspiration I had as a young woman – the worker priest movement in France, with its vision of Mass being celebrated at the kitchen table with fellow manual workers! My only links with my more radical past are through volunteering at the local foodbank and being an active member of the Friends of Erlestoke Prison. I justify my pleasant rural existence in a very beautiful place by thinking that this is my latest 'reinvention' in a life that has included several.

> Moving from city to city
> I have abseiled on ropes
> of friends
> hand over hand,
> phone calls and cards,
> visits made and received
> until returning to the new place
> was coming home.

6.
The time and space between

Janet Batsleer

> Hobgoblin, nor foul fiend
> Can daunt her spirit;
> She knows she at the end
> Shall life inherit.
> Then fancies fly away,
> She'll fear not what men say,
> She'll labour night and day
> To be a pilgrim.

I first sang this version of John Bunyan's poem at a service (in St Martin-in-the-Fields, perhaps; somewhere in London, certainly) that was held as part of the Movement for the Ordination of Women (MOW). I love singing it still. In this essay I want to explore a series of relationships to this movement and its consequences, as a woman with a very serious search and enquiry into faith and with a sense of belonging to the priesthood of all believers. I have chosen three moments in my life to offer a lens on this. The first is the moment of the women's liberation movement of the 1970s and 80s, when I was in my twenties. The second is the current moment in a much transformed Anglican

Communion, of which I, somewhat surprisingly, find myself a member, in a parish in Fallowfield, Manchester, dedicated to the Holy Innocents. The third is the in-between time, the long period of my involvement with women's studies teaching in higher education, with feminist approaches to youth work and community development, and with Womenspace and the Lay Women's Group that met at Freeland.

Significant themes that emerge from these reflections concern the desire for a transformation towards a more just and compassionate social order, the problem of the connection between church and wider social movements, and the need to place first the demand for and now the reality of the ordination of women within the context of those wider movements. But equally important is the issue of translation, mediation and connection between the different spaces within which I have lived these struggles as a lay woman. That my understanding has changed over a lifetime is a relief; I have not been fixed, rigid, static. That the transformations we have experienced in the whole global order have shifted all our understandings is a reality. But I return at the end of this piece to a book that I first reviewed for the magazine *Spare Rib* in 1983: Sara Maitland's *A Map of the New Country*.[1] We have been living in this new country for nearly forty years now. I wanted to revisit and reflect on how a map of its contours may have shifted; and on what remains challenging and contentious still.

1977–86

In the midst of the women's liberation movement, it was hard to hold on to an attachment to church (at least in my experience)

---

[1] Sara Maitland, *A Map of the New Country: Women and Christianity* (London: Routledge & Kegan Paul, 1983).

when free love became part of the powerful flow of a movement that was naming patriarchy and patriarchal controls as the enemy and Mary Daly was inviting us to go 'beyond God the Father'.[2]

I got married to Julian in 1975 at the beginning of my undergraduate degree. Between 1977, when I was finishing my degree, and 1989, when our son was born, I was utterly caught up in the women's liberation movement. I wasn't there at the start, but I was there near the start. I was alive with the need for and believed in the possibility of a socialist-feminist revolution. At the same time, I couldn't quite let go of the church (in my case the Church of England, whose Anglo-Catholic wing I encountered when I met Julian and then at university in Cambridge), and I was drawn to the revolutionary Marxist tendencies in the church, exemplified in the magazine *Slant*, edited by Terry Eagleton and other Roman Catholics, in liberation theology (though I found its theoretical frameworks hard to follow), and in the journal *New Blackfriars*, edited by radical Dominicans in Oxford. Eventually Julian and I found a raft to travel on for a while with the East London Jubilee Group, convened by Ken Leech, then parish priest at St Matthew's, Bethnal Green, and very prominent in the anti-racist, anti-fascist struggles of that era.

In this context, the outstanding need for reform in the rules governing ordination, represented by the Movement for the Ordination of Women in the Church of England, appeared as a liberal demand rather than being what we learned (from the far left) to term a 'transitional demand'. A demand, that is to say, which, in being met, would require the absolute transformation of the system. MOW seemed to be a hangover from the moment

---

[2] Mary Daly, *Beyond God the Father: Toward a Philosophy of Women's Liberation* (Boston, MA: Beacon Press, 1973).

earlier in the twentieth century when women had campaigned successfully for the vote and then immediately begun to campaign for and win access to the Civil Service and other professions from which they had been debarred. It seemed to be about equality with men of our own caste or class, rather than anything more revolutionary.

Nevertheless, the unhappy consciousness that had been raised by rubbing shoulders within the women's liberation movement, with the *Spare Rib* collective and with emerging feminist scholars did not disappear but made its unhappiness felt at the male dominance of the East London Jubilee Group. I also complained vociferously about the same patterns of dominance that emerged in Red Rope, the East London-based socialist walking and climbing club of which Julian, my husband, was a member.

On reflection, in the case of the East London Jubilee Group, this was, to a not insignificant extent, due to the dominance not of men in general but of one particular man who smoked a very particularly noxious pipe. A man who showed no awareness at all of the impact of this pipe either on himself or on others. Very much later, probably on the fortieth anniversary of the Ruskin Women's Liberation Conference, I learned that it had also been a dynamic of this nature that had led to the decision to make the Women's Liberation Conferences (which finished in 1978, so I did get to go to one) women-only spaces. This was because of the persistence of a particular male-dominated Maoist group who sought to instruct the gatherings, repeatedly and tediously, on the correct method by which to undertake a revolutionary struggle. The group has actually proved very helpful, as it was as a result of the interventions of this group that the Conferences had articulated a series of demands: starting with four and growing in number year by year to become the seven (or is it eight?) demands of the women's liberation movement. None of which included the right to be ordained as a priest within the Church of England or any other church, although they did of course include the demand for an end to sex discrimination in employment. But once this need for demands had been accepted, the persistent hectoring instruction seemed too much, and it was this, according to some accounts, that led to the decision to exclude men from the annual Women's Liberation Conferences.

In the 1970s I was a student and a part-time worker on London's Adventure Playgrounds, and in the 1980s I worked full-time as a youth and community worker until, after the defeat of the miners' strike, I took up a temporary post as a lecturer in youth and community work at Manchester Polytechnic. This provided me with gainful employment in what turned out to be a lifetime's work until my retirement in 2020. In the 1970s and 1980s, life on adventure playgrounds and as a cultural studies student seemed to be seamlessly part of the flux that was socialist politics and the women's movement. We lived on the outskirts, but my work was on the Islington/ Hoxton border before it was gentrified and I was in Central London at workshops, at socialist-feminist gatherings or just hanging out around Sisterwrite bookshop near Highbury and Islington station or at the Women's Research and Resources Centre at Embankment. I was a (very young) married woman and terrified – to an alarming degree – of encountering the lesbian presence in all those spaces. I was of course terrified, I now realise, of acknowledging my own same-sex desires (my and our understandings of both gender and of desire have been transformed over and over again since then). Also, somehow I was still hanging out with the church through our connection with the East London Jubilee Group and this felt part of being around the movement in London.

It was in fact through others involved in that group that I heard of some of the direct actions being taken in support of the Movement for the Ordination of Women. And I heard too, somehow – both through the group and also through an advert in *Spare Rib* – of the Women in Theology Conference that was being prepared at King's College, London. I offered a workshop on monogamy, and I was just as scared there as I was in Sisterwrite bookshop. If I was not a proper lesbian and therefore (it could seem) less of a feminist, neither was I a proper Christian any more.

I called myself a socialist-feminist, turned out for the Beyond the Fragments conference in Leeds, which proposed to rebuild the left on the basis of feminist principles of organising, did not consider the organising of women-only spaces as founding a separate/separatist movement but as a space of autonomy within the wider movement for change. I found the socialist-feminist movement a homely place because I was strongly committed to a socialist politics of building the long revolution away from capitalism, and was also beginning to embrace a wider understanding of the global dynamics of colonialism and imperialism on the lives of those from the former colonies living in or seeking entry to the UK. I struggled to make sense of an all-embracing concept of patriarchy, preferring the language of fighting sexism. However, it was also clear that a very significant presence in the cultural world that was forging new ways of living, establishing young women's centres, women's resource centres, bookshops and music groups was a lesbian community freshly claiming the word and the world. These were often women who were rejecting the male-dominated left. I did not belong here, however much I wished to. I wanted and needed to socialise and be with Julian, my male partner, and other comrades. But I did not 'fit' either in a straight heteronormative life. This much was clear.

Somehow my rock-climbing partner/husband and I stayed together and moved north just as the miners' strike and the Greenham Common Women's Peace Camp took up my weekends. We moved first to Sheffield (my birthplace), then to Wakefield and then to Manchester (near enough home for Julian). Apart from one important remaining connection with a cell group of the Jubilee Group – the Launde Abbey group, convened by Ken Leech, which met quarterly in retreat houses in which some enduring friendships were nurtured – I became an ex-Christian. However, my politics were focused on and nurtured by direct action: Greenham, Women Against Pit Closures, and anti-deportation campaigns, one of the most vital of which was the sanctuary established for Viraj Mendis in the Church of the Ascension in Hulme. I may have stopped being a Christian, but I had not stopped going to an Anglo-Catholic church.

2020: Holy Innocents, Fallowfield, Manchester

This is the church and parish where I have worshipped now for more than twenty years. I seem to have become an established pilgrim, perhaps too settled a seeker. It is a church in the 'liberal Catholic' Anglican tradition. It was built not long after the University of Manchester, in the late Victorian period, as a presence at the edge of the urban centre. The dedication to the Holy Innocents is an unusual one. It turns our attention consistently to those, especially the young, who are victims of violence and oppression, and the regular eucharistic celebration nurtures our hope that the persistence of violence and oppression will not have the final word.

The practices around which the life of the worshipping community is organised are worship, learning, solidarity and prayer. The contradictions that drove me away from church at the end of the 1980s are still present here, but this is a community in which the tensions and ambivalences are accepted as far as we are able; it does not shy away from difficulty or complexity. And it is a place and community in which I have over many years become able to use the word 'we'.

So, the language of worship remains patriarchal – but the churchwarden is a woman and a liturgist and a powerful influence in all aspects of the community's life. The language of hymns is inclusive; at the same time, we use the *English Hymnal*, whose emergence out of the late Victorian renewal of Anglican worship roots us in the period that the church was built. Worship is still centred on the Eucharist, which is celebrated much as it always was but now with women celebrants as well as men. Coming to 'the mysteries' week by week brings us together in a life that emphasises our shared participation in practices of thanks and praise, and that systematically turns us away from vengeance and violence as a response to violence and injustice. Conrad Noel, a famous early Anglo-Catholic socialist, once declared, 'Those who receive Holy Communion should be Holy Communists.' The sacramental declaration 'we are one body' becomes a source of reconnection to one another and to the prophetic life and journeying towards a world of solidarity, the world of the commons, the Commonwealth of God to come.

At times it is possible to see High-Church Anglicanism, even with all its understated upper-middle-class English culture, as a place of light and life to which many (myself included) who felt alienated from the church in the period of struggles concerning the ordination of women have joyfully returned.

At other times, though, we are torn apart by the struggles over ordination still: now the recognition of same-sex marriage and the suitability of those in same-sex marriages or civil partnerships for ordination. Our parish community lives with an openness to these issues at the same time as seeing people's sexual ethics and practices as an essentially private matter, and feeling discomfited when our difficulties and tensions over issues of sexuality seem to come to centre stage. It can become unbearable to be part of a wider church where this is still an issue, when we are a city church in Manchester, a city with LGBTQI+ communities at the forefront of opening up the current understandings of gender and sexuality.

This Anglican parish has also been a place of learning, both through the regular teaching and preaching of scholarly priests and in study groups and regular meetings concerned with faith and politics or peace and justice, which we as lay people have been supported in convening. This is a place of worship for people whose scholarship lies within theology and history but also within social science, literature and the arts. The methods of study are largely drawn from the adult education movement. They involve above all learning from one another as we journey along the way.

We have studied issues especially to do with fair trade, poverty, global justice and the arms trade. Despite the presence of strong feminists in the congregation, we have been less concerned to develop formally our understandings of intimate violence, sexual abuse and the abuse of children, though these subjects are never absent from our prayers. They emerge instead – as they do in many contexts – in the form of discussions of safeguarding practices for children and vulnerable adults in the church community, with which we are formally compliant, and in one-to-one support, which is by its nature kept confidential.

Increasingly, solidarity and prayer are understood as aspects of the same practice. Solidarity work has involved work for global justice, in support of fair trade and as part of the Jubilee Debt

Campaign. More recently we have begun to engage with issues of environmental justice. We have also made an active contribution to the Manchester networks in support of asylum seekers and refugees. Now a number of Iranian Christian converts have become an important part of our worshipping community.

From those who have arrived with us as asylum seekers, especially, I have learned a good deal about the ways in which faith communities can hold people as they cross borders. By some kind of accident, the houses behind our church, a terrace of what were once family houses and then were bought for students at Manchester University and became student lets, now have accommodation for the National Asylum Seekers Service (NASS). We had already supported asylum seekers as a community, in particular having been home to a very long campaign to achieve the right to remain for a Rwandan woman. Adela Mugabo was brought to church by Phil Tarbuck, a well-respected local activist in anti-racist and anti-deportation movements, and chair of Greater Manchester Immigration Aid Unit, who was also churchwarden at that time. Phil died in 2008, but the legacy of his life remained. We now have a community of forty Iranian, Kurdish, Afghan and Tajik Christians associated with the church, as well as other refugees from Cameroon. From accompanying these brothers and sisters, I have continued to learn about the systemic racism and deliberate systematically practised ignorance of the Border Agency, about the profound connections and challenges of the relationship between Islam and Christianity as communities of faith and practice, about the simple importance of being together, of finding connection and support, and about how the presence of trauma in a community is also a place where faith ignites and moves us to renewal.

I learned from a young age through experience and then

later in the time I was first involved with the East London Jubilee Group that turning to God in prayer and turning to actions of liberation and solidarity are not separate. Prayer and prophetic action, silence and solidarity, contemplation and resistance: this is the ground that we wish to nurture in the life of our parish community. Our dedication to Holy Innocents has led to us increasing our commitment to prayer in solidarity with people who face violence and persecution. The most recent form that this has taken has been in opening the church for contemplative prayer, a regular quiet place (in the eye of the storm) where we are trying also to find a way of being in stillness and silence with people of different faith traditions – Buddhists, Quakers, those interested in exploring different traditions of meditation and contemplation.

The in-between and elsewhere

I have a sense somehow that life beyond church has sustained these practices within it, and it is to this that I will turn in the final part of this essay.

In 1989 I became a mother, and around the same time I was given a permanent post as a lecturer. I found, in my dear friend Margaret, another life companion along the way, who, like me, was deeply formed by her early years in the Christian community, and alongside whom I returned to the practice of my faith. Margaret became our son Gregory's godmother. This period marked the end of my connection in any formal way with the Jubilee Group and the beginning of regular churchgoing. Somehow, as a result of this tangle of connection, Margaret and I found our way to meeting Hannah Ward and Jennifer Wild, and from there to our involvement with the Lay Women's Group that met in Freeland.

I remained committed to women's organising and to the

value of separate spaces for women, even while I knew that this was very far from the only basis for organising. I wrote about girls' groups as a method in informal education promoting connection, empowerment and autonomy, and I always gave a strong platform to lesbian perspectives in that work. This was part of an enduring thread of protest against the confines of heteronormativity. So, when the collective that came together to develop the short-lived women's studies MA at Manchester Metropolitan University emerged, I was energised once again, especially by developing a trans-disciplinary core course and by the commitment to making this postgraduate course an open access degree. My immersion in the Women's Studies project – as an extension of our autonomous feminist work with girls in youth work – led me over time to recognise that these feminist struggles could no longer be seen as adjuncts to struggles against the main enemy of, say, militarism or capitalism. Rather, I slowly realised that questions of the position and experience of women would raise the most profound questions about the nature of both politics and faith.

Working on this course also deepened my understanding of the importance of the recognition of difference and differing within social movements. It also gave me the confidence to return to reading theology, this time with a more certain affirmation that I would not abandon a questing and questioning after faith.

When the invitation came from Hannah and Jennifer to be involved with Womenspace events and then the Lay Women's Group, it was a very welcome opportunity to reflect on the strange fact that I seemed to have become an Anglican. I discovered that it was precisely for misfits like me that Womenspace came into being: for those who felt themselves as at the edge. As a result of meeting this group of women, my sense that the Movement for the Ordination of Women was not a radical movement needed to be, and has been, modified. I had signed up for and received a regular Women in Theology bulletin, but never fully recognised the importance of the women – including Bridget Rees, who was a key member of our Lay Women's Group – who were sustaining that work.

The Anglican Lay Women's Group offered me a way to reconnect with these questions. I was no longer a political activist in any formally organised way, other than in a trade union, but still deeply engaged by a feminist project that remained creative and was still generating counter practices in the field of youth and community work. From the parish, I was sustained by a regular participation in the Eucharist. In the connection with both the Community of St Clare, with its guest house (the Old Parsonage) and with the group that met there, I found complementary resources. In this group were women who had dedicated a large part of their lives to work in the church, in theological colleges, for Christian Aid, and within Franciscan religious communities. Most of them had also played important roles in the broadly defined Christian feminist movement, establishing for example the Women in Theology network and Womenspace. This small group of women has provided a context for me in which to explore faith and prayer, the pressing issues of the day, both personal (as we aged) and social and political. This enabled me to find living connection between aspects of my own life and experience that until then had seemed incommensurable. I believe that, nourishing though the life of the parish most certainly is, the existence of small groups such as this one, to one side of the institutional life of the church, is a necessary way to sustain a network of dissenting and prophetic life.

The existence of this women's group is in itself witness to the continuation under the radar of practices that Sara Maitland reported on in *A Map of the New Country*. It has been an open space of mutual support – dependent on the generosity of Hannah and Jennifer and of the Community of St Clare. The ethos of the group has been broadly egalitarian. It resembles most in its structure the Jubilee Group that Ken Leech convened, which met for a few years at retreat houses around England. But it has endured longer.

In 1983, Sara Maitland's book outlined the emerging shape of the territory we seemed to be entering. She began to explore the terrain to which the words 'Christian feminist' pointed and, as she was doing so, left clues for other explorers to pick up and follow. The chapter titles offer some signals: 'Women Together', 'Communities of Faith', 'Ordination', 'Women in the Bureaucracy' and 'Language and Spirituality'.[3]

These signals were certainly accurate pointers, and many of the themes have been widely engaged with over the ensuing forty years. But in many ways the book now reads as a warning about what is yet to come. Sara Maitland affirmed new emergent practices of women's collectives that might have much to teach the church about non-hierarchical forms of collaboration; she discerned the movement of the Spirit in the renewal of liturgy; and the exploration of language and creativity that no longer excludes the feminine from the divine. And she warned that a limited focus on ordination might be short-sighted. She argued that a lack of attention to the problems that arise when women take up roles in a bureaucracy (without at the same time seeking to change that bureaucracy) would be a thorn in the flesh of the movement.

There have been strong parallels in my experience between the ways in which women took up the priesthood in the Church of England and the professionalisation of

---

[3] Maitland, *A Map of the New Country*.

feminism within universities. Being 'priestly by function' or 'intellectual by function' and taking part in the community of practice with others who also share that position (clergy gatherings, academic conferences) tends to exclusivity and the development of codes and practices that maintain that exclusivity. Groups that cross such boundaries and seek to embed practices of mutual aid that take seriously ideas such as 'everyone is an intellectual' or 'priesthood belongs to all believers' are a necessary antidote to such exclusivity. The fact that we struggle for legitimacy and recognition is a sign of the power play still involved.

Translation and mediation

One of the most significant discussions that happened in the women's studies course arose from our readings of two American writers of first importance: Adrienne Rich and Donna Haraway. Rich was a poet who, on the one hand, affirmed so many aspects of difference – her Jewishness, her lesbian identity – and at the same time offered through her poetry and writing 'the dream of a common language'. Haraway is a scientist who has always engaged with both the new reaches of science and technology and with science fiction, fabulation and art. Her inspiring and difficult essay, 'A Manifesto for Cyborgs',[4] called for a women's movement that looked for 'an infidel heteroglossia: a speaking in many tongues'. The question of languages and tongues continues to preoccupy my thinking and my work. I increasingly hold the view that it is the practice of translation itself that is the common work and common language.

The language of Christian theologies and those of adult

---

[4] Donna Haraway, 'A Manifesto for Cyborgs: Science, Technology, and Socialist Feminism in the 1980s', *Socialist Review* 80 (1985), pp. 65–108.

education, community education and youth work can seem close at times, as certainly Christian understandings have influenced the development of practice in that field, both implicitly and explicitly. But the language of feminism as it has developed outside the church owes little to Christianity, and, indeed, as is the case with Donna Haraway's work, it explicitly and implicitly takes its distance from old patriarchal ideas of transcendence and associated forms of power.

The need to develop new languages and theorisations that more fully embrace difference, and the knots, nodes, links, chains of connectedness; the need to reimagine and remake our understandings of embodiment so that the (male = culture/ transcendence; female = nature/immanence) binary can be displaced and reworked; the need to find belonging and kinship and therefore kindness in affinity rather than family: all these are discussions with which the women's studies project in universities has engaged.

At the same time, I have regularly heard sermons in church that invite me to consider the presence of women (traditionally seen as unreliable witnesses) at the heart of the resurrection story or as central to Jesus' ministry; I have been invited to consider the significance of contemporary physics and genetics for our understanding of incarnation; and I have participated in Eucharists celebrated by lesbian, gay and trans priests. Yet these worlds are separate and I can feel as if I am their only point of connection. I am still searching for a common language, or else at least for an acceptance of a common need to become multilingual.

I find myself embarking on acts of translation and interpretation in crossing from one world to another. In the world of the Proud Trust, a north-west England youth project working with LGBTQI+ young people, I celebrate the queer presence in our church and speak of the importance of communities of faith to refugees and other 'new arrivals'. In the world of the church I laugh out loud and long at the idea that good sex is the preserve of heterosexual marriage. In the university I mention that the philosopher and mathematician A. N. Whitehead (currently in vogue) was a process theologian to whose work I was first introduced in a church youth group. I continually affirm the importance of the broken, the marginal and the dispossessed peoples as the chief sources for us in any chance we may have of understanding the meaning of the word 'love'. Blessed are the poor, for it is with them that we see rightly, and only with them that we will understand the meaning of our common ground.

And of course in church now, as nowhere else in my life, I am in a community of translators. The lessons and psalms are regularly read in Farsi. I see that script weekly and begin by ear to know the words for 'peace' and for 'Jesus Messiah' (Jesus Christ). I do not hide my membership of my church from those I encounter on other days of the week in my work, but it generally meets with bafflement. Neither do I hide my engagement with feminist, queer and anti-racist politics, practice and theory from those I meet in church: perhaps oddly there this is more welcome. But it has mainly been in the Lay Women's Group that I have found most interest in what I learn from these secular involvements. In a liminal space there is an opening – and, in that opening, who knows yet what may come.

This mid-life space, this space in the middle, the in-between, has been generative. I have very rarely held any kind of position in the church and I can feel that such faith as I have appears in disguise in my world of work and engagement. The hobgoblins and foul fiends are a more familiar presence in fairy stories than in the streets of Fallowfield. In the university we talk about 'the machine' as that which daunts our spirit, and I have studiously and deliberately avoided being part of 'the machine', both within the university and within the bureaucracy of the church, where I suspect many of the hobgoblins and foul fiends hide. The hobgoblins of patriarchal control of sexuality, as well as of abuse and violence, are familiar to me, and the foul fiends of both contempt and cynicism, despair and lassitude still daunt me. But being a pilgrim with others in the Lay Women's Group has shown me without fail (in the context of the women's movement in the church and outside of it) what it might mean to inherit life and to share in its abundance.

7.
Credo – or credon't
An attempt to make some sort of sense of my 'Christian' beliefs or lack of them
Frances Killick

Introduction

Outside Salisbury Cathedral there stands a beautiful statue of a woman walking purposefully (with her back to the cathedral), by Elisabeth Frink. I believe her official title is *Walking Madonna* but to me she is 'Everywoman' or indeed 'Anywoman' who is ambivalent about her relation to 'the church'.

For one who was confirmed in that same cathedral over sixty years ago and who attended its services (unwillingly) for nearly six years, that sculpture has tremendous meaning; for I feel that it was in the dreary years of compulsory church attendance as an adolescent at boarding school that the seeds of my questioning of the established church and all its works really germinated.

I am a 'cradle Anglican', christened when about six weeks old and taken to church regularly as a child. However, from the age of ten or thereabouts I felt there was something wrong about the picture of Christianity as presented by 'the church'. Before I was sure what 'virginity' meant, I had a feeling there was something that didn't add up – could I have been influenced by all those 'begats', which seemed to imply that Jesus was descended from King David via Joseph, or was the idea of his being the Son of God just incredible? Even then I disliked saying the Creed, as I felt hypocritical.

Later disconfirming influences were:

- The complete turn-off of the High Church-going at boarding school – an unknown and unexplained experience. Plus the (unfortunately) slobbering vicar who 'prepared' us for confirmation without coming near to where we might be starting from. With hindsight, the girls who resisted peer (and perhaps staff) pressure to be confirmed at 14 were braver and more independent-minded than most of us at that age!

- *Honest to God* – which came out soon after I graduated and just seemed like sense; but miles away from organised religion as I had largely experienced it.

- Christian feminism and the Movement for the Ordination of Women. The view of the church seen from these perspectives was not a positive one (see below, 'Hanging in or hanging out?').

- My 'rejection' (or at least a complete lack of welcome) by the church in Hemel Old Town when I started to attend there after moving to the area in the early 1980s.

On the other hand, there have been positive experiences:

- The solid Anglican tradition on both sides of my family (my great-grandfather, the rural dean; my great-grandmother, the pillar of the diocesan Mothers' Union, and so on).

Credo or credon't

- The statement by the evangelist Bryan Green, heard when I was 18, that following Jesus was like falling in love – sometimes 'at first sight', in an instant, at other times a much more gradual process. Since I have experienced both ways of falling in love, I could trust this analogy, even though I have never experienced an instant feeling of connectedness to Jesus. Sometimes I have felt helped by praying about things, but that's as far as it gets.

- Three wonderful university years at St Thomas's, Newcastle, when suddenly belonging to a church and its choir seemed to be such a good thing. This was probably also the beginning of my love of the heritage of church music I came to know; and culminated in a most enjoyable SCM summer school experience, particularly with the hymn writer Patrick Appleford as a tutor.

- Belonging to a church-related younger, single adults' group when I worked in the USA, which gave me many lifelong friendships and enjoyable experiences.

- Ten years at the Church of the Ascension, Blackheath, where the role and purpose of the church, as it existed for those outside it, made so much sense. The influence of the vicar, Paul Oestreicher, and the support of the local clergy when I had a serious illness were very important for me.

- Seven years with the Quakers of Hemel Hempstead – their 'sacramental' relationship with each other, a 'music in worship' meeting at Quaker Yearly Meeting (most unusual for the Quakers), their Peace Testimony (and going to Greenham Common), not having to sign up to any creed (except that of recognising that of God in every person). Their initial welcome was heart-warming and a wonderful contrast: 'Where have you come from?' 'I suppose I'm an Anglican refugee.' 'Oh, we're all refugees round here!'

So what does this add up to – after some seventy years of ambivalence?

I do believe that Jesus existed, although I think that a lot of the stories about him in the gospels are either based on myths or inserted in order to justify claims about who he was supposed to be. I am not sure that I can accept that he was the Son of God (and who 'God' might be is another huge question for me). I do not feel that I have a special relationship with Jesus. But I am comforted in this by having heard the former Bishop of Durham (David Jenkins) say that he only ever got 'whispers' direct from God, when asked if he had a 'hotline'. I understand that even Mother Teresa had her uncertainties and doubts.

I like to belong to a church (or a Meeting) as I find in such groups people whose values and ways of doing things accord with mine. I think I am a 'belonger' rather than a 'believer'. I have a great need to be useful to others (something one of my grandmothers wished for me when writing to congratulate my parents on my birth), which may well have influenced my decision to become a social worker. I have a liking for order and things being done properly – thus I am often a contributor to 'keeping the show on the road', even if I am not sure that it is a show that should continue!

The state of the Church of England/Anglican Communion makes me despair. How can people argue about questions of sexuality with so many people starving? Why are we not making a stronger witness about what is happening in Israel/Palestine? There are so many more important things. Can we really claim that the Gospel is 'good news', in view of the history of Christianity, the sexual abuse, the continuing sexism, homophobia, complacency, and so on?

I would like to talk about these ideas openly but have learnt to keep my mouth shut because of the reactions when I have mentioned them (even tentatively) in the past. Some of my worst church experiences have been when I have been asked to describe my 'faith journey', or something similar. This has usually led to someone offering to pray for me (which can feel like a hostile act in itself). But then I wonder – am I a hypocrite to go along with the general consensus and pretend I don't have such ideas? It's a lonely and uncomfortable place to be – especially as an officer of the deanery synod! However, recent articles and letters in the *Church Times* offer some comfort, as they indicate that others feel the same way about the churches' 'product' or 'offer' to the unchurched (in the whole climate of seeking 'growth').

Hanging in or hanging out?

My real emotional break with the church was not in the normal teenage upheavals (although I certainly dropped out for a time before committing myself to SCM and the church choir at university), nor over my theological problems. It was really over the ordination of women to the priesthood. One of the most frightening things I have ever done was to stand up in St Paul's Cathedral (during an ordination service) with seven others (in a protest organised by Monica Furlong), displaying banners demanding that women should also be ordained. We were ushered out, singing the Creed as we went, fully conscious of the might of church establishment and tradition! Then there was the day when a dozen deaconesses (as they were then) processed out of Southwark Cathedral during another ordination service. That was the day when I really 'detached' myself from the Anglican Church, and I have never been able to feel the same about it since, although I have subsequently worked in a diocesan post and have become quite involved in a parish church and local deanery, as well as chairing a town Churches Together organisation. In taking on such involvements, I think (again with hindsight) that I must have been seeking to reconcile my ongoing conflicts about Christianity. However, it is also true that I find the Church of England fascinating as an organisation (and the functioning of organisations is an area of great interest to me).

Life 'on the edge' has had its ups and downs: while some would consider it a wasteland, in my view the desert can come to 'blossom like a rose'. Such instances mainly happen for me in chances to meet for worship with other like-minded people, whether in women's groups or with women and men. The sad part is that such informal occasions have been (at best) unrecognised by the church as a whole, and (at worst) derided, disapproved of or actually prevented. Being 'at the margin' – a place where one obviously chooses to put oneself – is a strange experience; obviously one can get by on drinking skimmed milk (indeed, be a lot healthier for it) but full-cream milk tastes a lot better!

The good news is that one is not alone in being there: as time has gone on, it has become clear that there are many others who share a lot of the same views, as well as sharing the struggle to achieve the equality of men and women in the Church of England (by no means the same thing as women now being able to become priests and bishops). As a 'refugee' I have been grateful to find a spiritual home at times with the Quakers, but (like most refugees, perhaps) I long to go home again, although I wonder what 'home' means in this context. Sometimes when I experience wonderful choral music in the context of a service, I wonder why some people should feel obliged to cut themselves off from such sources of comfort and strength. Equally, there are so many sources of anger at the way both lay people and clergywomen are treated when they are involved in church worship and activities that it is hard to remain. The central question seems to be how to be true to your ideals and principles, and yet also remain true to rightly honoured and valued traditions.

Christian feminism and the future

Given this personal background, I would now like to consider some ideas about Christian feminism and the future. With the recent development of the 'new feminism' (such as it is), it seems a good time to try to assess this, and it has been encouraging to see the appearance of several relevant books and articles within the last few years.

Christian feminists are not a particularly homogenous group (in fact many women would probably be reluctant to identify themselves under this generic term). Some people (mostly now gone) struggled for years to promote the cause of the ordination of women, and it seems almost unbelievable that they could have kept going with such minimal success and yet remain so loyal to the organisation that gave them so little. The tone of the legislation that was eventually passed in the General Synod was so grudging, so concerned with safeguards for those who might find the circumstances of their employment changed, that it became hard to see why any women bother to stay with the church at all. But perhaps it's like a bad job situation: somehow staying on may be better than facing the (imagined or, indeed, real) cold employment world outside. Some women cannot face an uncertain work situation on their own (for whatever reason), even suffering bullying and sexism and the abuse of unequal pay, rather than leaving for an uncertain future. I have been in this situation myself, but was fortunate that it happened at a time when I could be reasonably sure of finding a new post quite quickly (also I had no mortgage at the time).

Obviously such uncertainty is not true of many women who have left, and who continue to leave the Church of England (and indeed the other churches). Listening to a group of women at one of the meetings that used to be offered by (for example) Womenspace (see Chapter 2), it was clear that there were many women around who shared a deep ambivalence about organised religion and their former loyalties, but who were also very conscious of their ongoing spiritual needs. Credal statements often seem totally inadequate to express these needs for belief, if only because they feel far too definite to allow for day-to-day fluctuations in individuals' convictions! Evangelically based organisations may expect those working for them or joining them to sign up formally to their beliefs, but the C of E as a whole does not exercise such means of control. The unspoken assumptions and practices may weigh quite heavily at times, but the Church of England is, emphatically, not like (for example) the Brethren.

Over the years, many networks and organisations have been set up to relate to these needs, and to women's exclusion from the traditional sources of power in the churches; obviously these groups have varied in their purposes and their outcomes. Some have achieved their goal/s and have closed down, others have simply withered away. I know I am not alone in having continuing sadness (and indeed anger) over the failure (due to financial and organisational problems) of Websters (the women's spirituality centre set up in Central London in the early 1990s).

I am conscious that many (but certainly not all) of the women who take part in the various groups could be described as 'older women', and I therefore wonder what the future of such activities will be. Obviously this is true of many churches as well (although they also contain some older men), and one can equally well speculate about their future. Of course there is nothing wrong with older women (being one myself), and there are many good reasons why younger women do not have the time to become involved in women's spirituality groups – but will they want to when they do have the time? Perhaps whole new ways of satisfying one's spiritual needs, which cannot yet be imagined, will emerge – but somehow I do not think it will be through the traditional churches unless they are prepared to change in very radical ways.

One of these ways is the need for a much more committed approach to issues of social justice. There is such a vast gap between the rhetoric used and the reality experienced here. It seems obvious that many, perhaps most, church people do not want to be challenged or made uncomfortable by the needs of the poor and the marginalised; nor do they want to try new ways of doing things. It would seem, indeed, that many people go to church in order to be affirmed and emotionally 'stroked', in remaining in their comfortable patterns. This was the real reason why I gave up my diocesan job as an advisor in social responsibility. The role was basically about 'awareness raising', and if people do not want to become more aware it's hard to remain convinced of the usefulness of one's work.

One might have hoped that some of the interesting developments in feminist theology would offer some paths forward here, but on the whole this does not seem to be the case. Until recently I would certainly not have dared even to consider this material the stuff of feminist theology. However, after I joined a feminist theology reading group, I wondered why so much feminist theology seems to be so divorced from women's experience, being in the academic mode. Is this because the only way to achieve 'success' and recognition is to join the system? Has feminist theology been 'hijacked' from its origins in women's experience? No answers, I am afraid – but maybe it's worth trying to continue thinking about some of the questions.

I would like to continue this chapter by returning to the personal, as I believe that a feminist's own theology can only evolve from their personal experience. In one period of struggle with my own confusion I was heartened by a day school on feminist theology that I attended in Oxford. At the end of the afternoon, Jane Shaw (the main speaker) was asked how she saw the future of feminist theology. She made two suggestions that seemed helpful. The first was that feminist theology should become 'gender theology' (an insight that seems long overdue to one with a degree in gender studies – but elaborating on that would need another chapter). The second was that, rather than leaving the churches, maybe women should try to stay with them, in the hope of changing them from the inside rather than complaining about their practices from the margins. This is, of course, the old argument about the most effective way to achieve change and begs the question, 'Yes, but how?'

Some ways of coping

I would like to share some of the strategies I have found (and, as one who has held some responsibility in the local ecumenical scene, I certainly have needed them). I hope that they don't sound too obvious.

- Not trying to 'go it alone': finding companions for the journey, people with whom I can express my own doubts, anxieties and feelings without fear of what others might say if they knew my views. Non-credal religious organisations such as the Quakers, and alternative groups such as those that were publicised by Women in Theology (WIT), can be good sources of such companions. However, I do have to be prepared to put some time and energy into sharing the lives of these groups if I expect to get something out of them, and this can be difficult if I am also trying to remain within the church fold.

- To deal with this (potential if not actual) conflict of loyalties, it is necessary to be very clear about priorities, especially when this means standing up to partners and other family members or friends, who find what one is doing incomprehensible. It can be a case of compromise in some circumstances ('Yes, I will do this, but not that'); it will require careful organisation, and there may be financial implications (for example, in relation to giving to churches or charities, and in spending on transport). Guilt is endemic in this situation – but then which of us does not live with guilt of some sort most of the time, given the circumstances of our 'comfortable' lives?

- I try not to worry about not doing things as I would really like to do them. One helpful (if somewhat patronising) comment I once heard a friend's husband make was, 'Why do you girls always have to be so bloody perfect?' In a sense, he had a point. Perhaps anxieties over needing to be liked, and the consciousness of wanting to do things 'properly' (in an inclusive way), can tie our hands too much. It can sometimes be helpful to try to remember that we can't 'be all things to all people all the time' (not without driving ourselves into some sort of breakdown), and that 'we can't win 'em all'.

• If I find I really cannot cope with some religious practice or demand, such as 'giving a personal testimony', I do not try to force myself to take part in it, knowing that I will only become angry and frustrated – with others, with myself and (perhaps) even with God (who/whatever I may think about God at that point). I try instead to think out my position before the event and work out what I am going to do or say before I get sucked into the situation: for example, preaching is not my thing (and I don't find many sermons valuable either), so I must not let myself fall into assumptions made by others that I will preach on certain occasions.

• I find that reading can be very helpful. Some journals in particular can make me feel less alone in my views, for example (the former) *Christian* and Sea of Faith journals, and some theological works, such as many of Daphne Hampson's books and those by Richard Holloway.

Conclusion

Writing and revising this essay has been a cathartic experience although not one that has (as yet – see below) led to any real resolution of my doubts! It has been completed in the later stages of the first COVID-19 so-called 'lockdown' experience, which has disrupted the lives of all of us. There has been a lot of comment about whether things will be different once the acute stage of the pandemic is over. How may this affect the churches? Some have been very actively involved in social and community projects, supporting foodbanks and so on during this period, but others will not have changed their assumptions about their usual role. There has certainly been a growth in awareness of the current inequalities in our society, but will this result in any greater willingness to take action rather than call for yet more reports on the part of government or churches? After all, any social or community worker could have produced plenty of evidence about the dire state of many communities, families and individuals known to them over the last ten years!

However, this is not a professional social work or academic report but a personal one. So, where does my attempt to understand my Christian beliefs, or lack of them, and to explain them to myself, or indeed to others, leave me? I certainly feel more justified in my ambivalence – which is a more comfortable place to be; and it is good to know that many others (some very eminent) have had similar doubts and concerns. So, maybe it is all right still to be in a state of uncertainty here. If I have learnt one thing from the constraints imposed by Covid-19 and my current health problems, it is the need to accept compromises and not to fret over things I would prefer to be different. I probably cannot help how my views on life have been shaped but I can learn to live with these views.

My final paragraphs must be to remind myself of yet another way of coping with being 'on the edge', not mainstream. Don't take yourself too seriously! This was once beautifully illustrated for me during a session of the Lay Women's Group at Freeland when I was agonising over my doubts about saying the Creed. One colleague helpfully reminded me it was only a statement of the church's agenda, and another that what she believed in was regular meals! Alleluia! Amen to that!

I am very grateful to the other members of our Lay Women's Group for their support and friendship over the years when we have met together. They must have got tired of hearing me wittering on about my difficulties over questions of faith and belief. I am particularly grateful to Janet Batsleer and Margaret Beetham for their helpful feedback on an earlier draft of this essay.

8.
Who can find a virtuous woman?

Margaret Halsey

In this article I explore aspects of my work as a lay woman in church-based
employment, making some links with liturgy, music, songs and hymns that
have inspired me on the way, and weaving in some threads from a wider
background context in education, politics and theology.

Throughout my childhood, springtime was associated with a burst
of flowers – primroses on green banks, daffodils and narcissi in
the large garden, lambs being born in fields nearby, and watching
the Boat Race and the Grand National on the small TV in the
corner of our sitting room. All this was inextricably linked with
Lent, which started with that reminder of forty days and forty
nights when Jesus was fasting in the wild, and the rather more
pious hymn 'Christian, dost thou see them'. Its words indicated
that the hosts of Midian prowled and prowled around. I did not
at that stage have a clue who the hosts of Midian were, and at the
age of ten I did not like to ask, so I sang along and hoped I did not
come into contact with the prowlers. I was more at home singing
about Robin Hood.

Finally we reached Good Friday and its three-hour service

where we were reminded that there is a green hill far away without a city wall. My father, as the rector of an affluent Surrey village, led a three-hour service of reflections punctuated by hymns and prayers. My mother took me and my brother along for the last hour. For years I thought the city had no wall until I discovered that the green hill was outside the city wall. My most vivid recollection was that we all took sugar lumps as my father was diabetic and there was a possibility that he might go into a coma. So the best parts for me about Good Friday were hot cross buns and the evening meal of fish pie topped with mashed potato.

On Saturday I often went up to church again to decorate it, joined by my mother and a number of women from the church. She always looked for a small window as she was 'not much of a flower arranger'. Finally we reached Easter when hymns were much more joyful. My happiest memory was of all the children being invited to go and sit in the sanctuary in order to make room for a rather larger congregation than usual. We always started by singing 'Jesus Christ is risen today', which I found rather repetitive with alleluias that went on for a long time, and I preferred 'This joyful Eastertide, away with sin and sorrow', which struck me as much more fun. In the last hymn there was an Easter offering in the collection to thank my father for what he did, and later a discreet conversation between my parents when we got home about how much it had raised! My older brother and I made ourselves scarce to crack open an Easter egg.

The Easter season was a working one as far as we were concerned. So I much enjoyed the week afterwards when we usually had a holiday in Wales, courtesy of a parishioner who owned a cottage on the Gower Peninsula. It was always a lovely time as we got to play on a beach, often in the wind and rain. I learnt enough Welsh to say good morning, good afternoon and good night, which Tom, a local man who made his living as a gardener, had taught me.

Looking back, I realise that many of these memories have deeper symbolic meanings of Easter themes: of death and new life, of suffering and hope, of the garden of Gethsemane and the tomb in the garden where Jesus was buried, of hot cross buns, roast lamb, fish and eggs and their significance for Christian belief and practice. Of course my theological views about the crucifixion and resurrection have changed radically since then, but the symbolism has stayed with me.[1]

In the church I now attend in inner-city Leeds, we hold an Easter vigil and confirmation. A fire is lit in a brazier outside, while traffic rushes to and fro on the busy road into the city. The Easter candle is lit and carried at the head of a procession, and a solo 'The light of Christ' is sung as we respond 'Thanks be to God' and move inside. Slowly but surely, we light our candles from it and pass the light from one to another. I begin to make some sense of Christ's wounds being imprinted on the candle, of my own journey, which has inevitably involved suffering and hope, and that of the wider world in which we are constantly reminded of the need for renewal and healing in the face of injustice and conflict.

As someone who initially came from a 'liberal evangelical' background I am surprised by how much I love the swinging of incense. Perhaps this is because I have always enjoyed its smell when I visit Greek Orthodox churches on holidays. Now the symbolism of the worship in my current church speaks to me of God's mystery, and the busy road outside speaks to me of 'being

---

[1] Mary Douglas, in her book *Natural Symbols: Explorations in Cosmology* (London: Penguin, 1969), explores aspects of dietary customs about Easter in the Roman Catholic tradition from an anthropological perspective.

the church' in a city inhabited by people of all faiths and none. As one of a team of people who run a class on Sundays for all who are new to the Christian faith, many of whom are asylum seekers, my task has often been to ensure confirmation preparation is done well, so I am always moved by the service.

The decades that separate those two very different celebrations have been important in discovering how, as a lay woman, I experienced employment in ecumenical or Anglican organisations. The hardest decade for me to relive is the 1960s when, because my mother had breast cancer, I was sent away to a girls' boarding school so I would have a community where I belonged, and could get on with the task of doing my O and A levels. In one way, that was a huge privilege and a very 'rounded' education, but in another I found it bewildering to be mixing with others who were far more sophisticated than I was, and rather richer.

At the time, I saw my mother as the disciplinarian in the family, but I now realise she was the person who made us all think. I well recall one Sunday lunch on Mother's Day when she shared her take on the biblical reading, 'Who can find a virtuous woman?' She told us all that she did not remotely fulfil the domestic requirements, nor was her price far above rubies, which provoked a very lively and humorous conversation. I also recall the time around one election when she sat looking at a party political broadcast given by Hugh Gaitskell. When I expressed surprise, as we lived in a safely Conservative constituency, her immediate reply was, 'I wonder if it is more Christian to vote socialist.' It was my mother too who told us all that she was very politically moved by watching people of different racial origins sitting down together in a square in Washington DC and singing 'We shall overcome' when Martin Luther King had delivered his speech 'I have a dream'.

Who can find a virtuous woman?

When my mother died, my father and brother came down to the school to break the news, and a place was made for us to have lunch in private. I was asked if I wanted to go home for the funeral but, never having been to a funeral before in my life, I decided against. Later, the decision left me with a sense of inappropriate guilt, but more importantly I discovered it was vital to say goodbye to a person, place or situation well in order to move on.

My confirmation took place quite soon afterwards, and I recall kneeling in front of a large, kindly looking bishop who bent over to put his hand on our heads while the congregation were singing 'Come, Holy Ghost, our souls inspire'. I certainly felt slightly haunted by this ghost, had no idea what a soul was, and was not quite sure what I was being inspired to say or do except be 'lightened with celestial fire'. My godparents, father and older brother all made the effort to come down to support me and, as we were all very conscious that my mother was not there, I was very grateful they had done so.

A couple of years later, I left school and went to Edinburgh University to study biological sciences. I loved student life and the city, and was very impressed by the clarity of the lectures on genetics in my first year, given by Professor Charlotte Auerbach. Later I discovered she was Jewish and had fled Nazi Germany to pursue her PhD. She excited me about the subject and I immediately decided that it was the area I wanted to study for my honours degree. Four years included two modules in the history and philosophy of science, which stretched my mind, enabled me to think around the ethical implications of studying science, and gave me a rigorous understanding of its social context.

My father had suggested I might want to be involved with SCM as the Christian Union was 'rather more devout' and 'might not be quite my cup of tea'. So I happily trundled along to SCM meetings on Friday evenings, absorbed the wisdom of thought-provoking theologians from Edinburgh's School of Divinity, and talked endlessly into the night at a discussion group with others from different university faculties. The theological world became far more dynamic and interesting, and introduced me to a wide range of new perspectives. Musically it was the era of the Beatles, whom I loved to bits, particularly the song 'Here Comes the Sun' and the album *Sgt Pepper's Lonely Hearts Club Band*. In my first term I had enjoyed being in a choir that sang Mozart's Requiem. However, at that stage of my life, religious music featured less than selected pop, folk and social justice songs.

In 1969, I travelled to Manchester in the SCM minibus to a student congress of more than fifteen hundred students making links between Christianity, race and poverty. The experience of hearing Dom Helder Camara, the Roman Catholic Archbishop of Recife in Brazil and an advocate of liberation theology, was to me the nearest experience to a 'conversion' I have ever had, and we stood to applaud him for ten minutes. I recall him as a small, quiet man talking to us in a clear and humbling style, and this had a lasting effect on my final two years at university and subsequent paid work.

At that point I did not attach myself to any church, but enjoyed occasional visits to the chaplaincy and the Quakers when I wanted to explore different styles of Christian spirituality. Both places, along with SCM, provided me with a sense of stability in a life that felt quite personally unstable. I needed to have a sense of belonging in a situation where my family was being completely changed by my brother marrying and my father remarrying. In one summer break I discovered the Iona community in a minibus trip led by the chaplain from Dundee University. In another, I visited the Taizé community where its musical tradition extended my understanding of prayer. Singing in a different language took me out of myself into an inspirational sense of transcendence, otherness and mystery.

The next decade was one in which I graduated from university, was offered a very stimulating job with the Christian Education Movement (CEM) in Scotland, moved to the Midlands, and ended up as a lay chaplain to Brighton Polytechnic. The joy of all the work was that it was ecumenical and worked across denominational boundaries. When working for CEM I learned much about belonging to different kinds of teams, the breadth of religious education and its underlying rationale, and how to design conferences and courses. In Scotland I had mainly worked with sixth-form conferences, and in the Midlands the work was broader, servicing RE teachers and working with both primary and secondary schools, and I learned much more about faith development.[2]

I was also asked to write and publish material for RE, including something on medical ethics, and I much enjoyed the chance to design simulation games that broadened learning from being a question of imparting knowledge from teacher to student to one where people learned from a shared experience. This later became central to my understanding of adult education where clergy and laity could learn from one another. I became more aware of the variety of faiths in Britain, which stretched my mind considerably.

---

[2] Nicola Slee's book *Women's Faith Development: Patterns and Processes* (Aldershot: Ashgate, 2004) offers an overview of the process of faith development, which during the time I was working largely referred to the work of Jean Piaget and James Fowler. She explores how understandings of the process of women's faith have developed more recently, and in a final chapter she looks at the implications of this for both Christian education and pastoral practice. Anne Phillips' book *The Faith of Girls: Children's Spirituality and Transition to Adulthood* (Aldershot: Ashgate, 2011) is based on interviews with adolescent girls aged 11–14 in large-, medium- and small-sized urban congregations and explores their varied understandings of spirituality using biblical texts to which they could relate.

Edgewise?

The post in the Midlands was based in the offices of Coventry Cathedral. I continued to sit fairly light to churchgoing but much enjoyed the cathedral's beauty and contemporary design. Occasionally I went to an early morning ecumenical service in the Chapel of Unity on Wednesdays. The modern cathedral is built alongside the ruins of the one that had been bombed during the Second World War. It was a powerful sight to ponder on my route to work and made me wonder what it would have been like for those who experienced their city being bombed. Later in life, I learned of the time when the Coventry Carol was sung in the ruins of the bombed cathedral at Christmas in 1940.[3]

By the time I arrived in Brighton where I had been offered a job as chaplain to the polytechnic in 1979, I realised that the hymns I could sing with integrity were less prescriptive about belief and more sensitive to issues of social justice. It was a standing joke among us all that my attempts at making texts more inclusive sometimes resulted in rather odd scansion, and looking back I realise that my male clergy colleagues were remarkably open-minded. In the polytechnic I was the only woman on the team, and in the wider higher education team there was also a Catholic nun. Although we liked one another, our attitudes about gender and our theological views were very different.

Initially we held an Anglican celebration of the Eucharist in the chaplaincy centre, where I lived with four or five students, but later moved to the university Meeting House to join a wider ecumenical congregation. I was on the rota for preaching, which was a remarkable challenge, but I learned as I went along. There were a number of very gifted preachers on the team. Preaching was one of the tasks my father had much enjoyed and I informally

---

[3] The Coventry Carol originated in the sixteenth century and featured in a mystery play performed in Coventry. It was sung by three women of Bethlehem and laments the massacre of the Innocents.

learned a lot from his style. The service brought together people who had very different views of life to stand alongside one another when we received the bread and wine, but we were also aware how ecumenically divisive the celebration could be. So I particularly enjoyed working with my Roman Catholic colleagues, who taught me much about their tradition.

Working in the polytechnic science-based building gave me a chance to do some lecturing in an area of science and ethics. I also much enjoyed working with the senior careers counsellor to explore aspects of its hidden curriculum in a conference for polytechnic staff. This drew together people from several departments, offering an opportunity to reflect on values in higher education and share ideas about wider policy decisions.[4]

As I got to know various staff better, some began to talk about why their experience of religion had alienated them from churches. It was a great privilege to be trusted in that way. I was occasionally called upon to work with students who were for a range of reasons distressed by their experience and/or their sexuality, so I enrolled on a diploma course to qualify in counselling and group dynamics. My dissertation on feminism and counselling brought me into contact with all sorts of writing, which excited and challenged me in a range of different ways. I wondered whether to apply for counselling work and move out of church employment, but for various reasons that door did not open up easily.

One highlight of that period was the opportunity to go to Greenham Common in the time I would be taking off work. It

---

[4] The term 'hidden curriculum' originated in the writing of Ivan Illich and refers to underlying values about learning in educational institutions in Latin America. It is explored more extensively in his book *Deschooling Society* (London: Calder and Boyars, 1971).

was good to stand outside with others singing 'No cruise missiles wanted here today' to the tune of 'Ten green bottles hanging on the wall', and it was an extraordinarily moving experience to link arms and ring the whole fence singing 'We are gentle, angry people'. I did not have the desire to camp there myself, nor could I do so given the day-to-day working demands. But I felt it was important to show a sense of solidarity with those who did, and to see a nuclear base.

My life in Brighton was enriched by a small women's support group where four of us met for an evening meal every six weeks and talked in confidence about our work. We all came from the welfare area of the polytechnic, and the meeting I remember most vividly was when we all made a pact to record our dreams for a month and explore what they might mean. I shared one about Iranians in the basement, although I have no idea now what the dream was or how it was interpreted. But I well remember that one of the group subsequently bumped into me in a corridor and quietly asked how the Iranians were doing. The conversation took place in stage whispers, and we looked furtively over our shoulders to ensure no one was listening in.

I left Brighton in the middle of the next decade to work as an industrial missioner based in South Yorkshire. I had been phoned about the job by one of the women on the team and knew it would be very challenging. I had rattled buckets for the striking miners outside Sainsbury's and decided to apply as I had no idea what it would be like to be based in northern industrial England. Although industrial mission's origins are in the male-dominated industries of coal and steel, I was assured that there was a continuing commitment to working with women as well as men. So I arrived at the interview with my head full more of questions than answers, stayed with a friend overnight, and was offered the job. It seemed to me that this was the 'next right place to be', which is how I make some sense of 'vocation'.

Inevitably it was a huge culture shock, and I was glad of the training I was offered. I attended several courses that explored aspects of industrial mission and one to gain a diploma in practical theology. I had the sense of being part of a tradition that for me was developed by the lay theologian Margaret Kane. She wrote three books weaving together her experience as an industrial missioner and her subsequent work as theological consultant to churches in north-east England.[5]

I am reasonably sure that when I first visited British Steel the men who worked there wondered how long I would last. When I arrived on a course about trade unions I was advised that I would have to learn how to flatten my vowels. I was also told by someone not to bring a Bible in my pocket – an idea that had never occurred to me at all. But I knew I had got over various unseen hurdles after a couple of years when one of the trade union representatives remarked that 'the lads' had said to him, 'What if she doesn't like the girlie posters?' and he had told them, 'Look lads, this is a steelworks not a nunnery.' I have written more about some of the ways in which I was affected and changed in the book *Life Cycles: Women and Pastoral Care*, which I co-edited with Elaine Graham.[6]

To counterbalance the work I was doing in Rotherham Engineering Steels I was invited to a working women's group where we listened to the women's experiences of low-paid work and how they juggled this with domestic commitments. When I studied for an MA in Hull, my dissertation research enabled me

---

[5] See Margaret Kane's three books: *Theology in an Industrial Society* (London: SCM Press, 1975); *Gospel in Industrial Society* (London: SCM Press, 1980); and *What Kind of God?* (London: SCM Press, 1986).
[6] See 'Crossing the boundaries', in *Life Cycles: Women and Pastoral Care*, ed. Elaine Graham and Margaret J. Halsey (London: SPCK, 1993).

to learn much more about the implications of contracting out cleaning work in schools, including its theological interpretation. All this in turn led to my learning about how traditional expectations of the nature and context of women's work might be carried over into wider employment practice. An edited version of this research was later published.[7]

I enjoyed being part of a diverse ecumenical team whose regular meetings were very lively. A variety of initiatives were being taken by colleagues to develop projects with unemployed people and training schemes for younger people. We had a commitment to work with a variety of churches in the field of theological education and were often asked to preach and/or take services in the area. I was very glad to have another woman to talk with informally about the work. When she moved on and I was the only woman on the team, it was harder to hold my own ground.

In 1994 the Industrial Mission in South Yorkshire (IMSY) celebrated its fiftieth birthday and I can well recall the tea party we held in Sheffield City Hall to draw a wide range of folk together to celebrate. I had decided to write a song about its history, which the staff agreed to sing to the tune of 'On Ilkley Moor Baht 'at'. The inspiration to do so was the result of research and writing by Paul Bagshaw, a staff member of IMSY from 1986 to 1990.[8]

This task was rather simpler than being part of the team who were negotiating and designing the celebration service in the cathedral the following evening, where we needed to ensure it represented our geographical spread, variety of work and ecumenical diversity. We had commissioned a hymn for the

---

[7] An edited version of the text was later published by the William Temple Foundation in 1996 and entitled *Invisible Hands*.

[8] Paul Bagshaw, *The Church Beyond the Church: Sheffield Industrial Mission 1944–94* (Sheffield: Sheffield Design and Print, 1994).

occasion, and at the Offertory it was very moving to see people bring up symbols of their lives at work, and the projects where unemployed people were finding ways forward. The sermon preached by Christa Springer, who was the director of the urban industrial mission centre in Mainz, drew on a reading from the wisdom tradition, reminding us of what we were learning from being part of a wider European network.

In this period the vote to ordain women went through the General Synod, much to the delight of the group of us who joined the local Movement for the Ordination of Women (MOW), where its meetings were both business-like and fun. Yet although I had no doubt that the possibility of priestly ordination of women was a matter of justice, I saw no reason why my own work necessarily needed to be done by someone who was ordained.

During my time in the Diocese of Sheffield a group of us met together to explore themes in worship and produce short liturgies, which was another important part of a support network. My interest in inclusive worship came alive and complemented the work the industrial mission did as a team when we were invited to take services and/or preach in local churches.

At the end of ten years' work in industrial mission and a sabbatical when I travelled in India, a post came up as director of laity development in the Diocese of Manchester. I was offered the job, so had a leaving service in my local church followed by a party. I devised the service, drawing on material from the Iona community to take account of the very diverse group of people who would attend, and I preached the sermon. The music reflected many of the ideals we had lived out in industrial mission. The music I most remember was 'She sits like a bird brooding on the waters', linking aspects of the wisdom tradition with the start of creation, and a South African chant, sung during the intercessions, both in its original language and in English.

The subsequent party was a complete one-off. A highlight for me were the two men, retired from work in steel and coal and part of the congregation, who had dressed in drag and sang 'Sisters'. One was so well disguised that only when I was hauled on to the stage to join them did I realise who it was, and collapsed in laughter.

The work in which I was involved in Manchester was a strong contrast to that which I had done in South Yorkshire – not least because I had made a decision to move back into work that was initially 'church based' rather than 'world based'. At the time, several reports were circulating about the area of laity development, and there were a number of books that were very influential in developing its theory and practice. The numbers of people attending church worship were declining, wider society was becoming more secularised and pluralist; there was as always a tension between mission and maintenance within the churches. All these factors affected the ways in which lay people were involved in local congregations.[9]

The Diocese of Manchester was industrially based on cotton, spinning and weaving, and divided into three very different areas in which to work. One of the aspects of the post that I most enjoyed was to develop and pilot a course that could be used across the diocese, entitled 'Living and Learning' and consisting of three modules – Believing, Belonging and Becoming. Because the group of people with whom I worked came from varied church backgrounds, we offered a wide variety of material and ensured it took account of different learning styles. We agreed a structure of the course before we began; it was relatively straightforward

[9] There are many reports that offer an overview of how laity interact with church life. Two key texts in the area are John M. Hull, *What Prevents Christian Adults from Learning?* (London: SCM Press, 1985), and Yvonne Craig, *Learning For Life: A Handbook of Adult Religious Education* (London: Continuum, 1995).

to weave together the material, and benefited much from two adult educators from the department of continuing education at Manchester University.

The post also gave me the opportunity to develop some collaborative material in the area of pastoral care with a well-qualified ordained local minister. On one of the most telling evenings I spent in a parish, the lay people who had been asked by their parish priest to meet me did not think they had any relevant qualifications. So I asked them about the skills they used at work, and it became very clear that these were highly relevant and transferable. 'But many people say that pastoral care doesn't really count unless the vicar is there' was their next assertion. So I indicated that some parishes had held a licensing service to ensure that these assumptions were gently challenged and that they were properly authorised.

Because of the ecumenical contacts made in my previous work I was able to contribute to the education of people preparing for ordination in the Free Churches, based at Luther King House in Manchester. Together with the area officers for laity development, I ran a number of events that explored spirituality and working life, and with colleagues from the field of social responsibility I was part of a team exploring the theme of spirituality in the city. What I found most satisfying of all was being able to run parish away-days and have the opportunity to get to know a parish in more depth.

The church I attended during my time in Manchester was one where I was made very welcome, almost immediately felt at home with many of the people who went there, and found it helpful to sit in the congregation and be nourished by its life. As life in the diocesan office had not always been easy it was good to have a base where I had no need to justify my existence. I had also been invited to a ritual group based in Manchester where we were exploring aspects of transition in women's lives. So when the diocese had a shortfall in its budget and a number of posts were made redundant, including the one I occupied, this group was a place where I could devise a ritual, honestly explore some of my feelings, link them with wider experiences of grief and bereavement within the group and look to the future. Two hymns/songs that stand out from this time in my life were 'There's a Wideness in God's Mercy', which was sung at a close friend's funeral, and 'Deep Peace of the Running Wave to You', which we sang at the end of the ritual.[10]

The ritual definitely gave me a sense of being more 'in charge' of the situation and, having put in various job applications, I was called for an interview the following week. When I had wandered into the SPCK bookshop below the office, the hymn 'Lord for the Years, your Love has Kept and Guided' was playing in the background. Much to my surprise I was offered the job as Director of the Leeds Church Institute (LCI), undoubtedly the most challenging work I have ever done. I was well qualified and experienced in the area of adult education, making links between city life and aspects of faith, and leading voluntary staff teams, but I had a lot to learn about personnel management, developing a strategic vision for the work, ensuring a large building was well managed, and various aspects of charity governance.

During my period in office the trustees decided to call in an external work consultant to help us restructure the organisation so that it was 'fit for purpose', which was not a popular move with some of the staff. I had to weather the storm that broke and ensure that we stayed within the limits of charity law when we

---

[10] See 'Case Study Three', in Jan Berry, *Ritual Making Women: Shaping Rites for Changing Lives* (London: Continuum, 2009).

were reorganising. By the time the process was complete – I had rewritten all the job descriptions, negotiated two compromise agreements and reappointed new staff – I needed some time off work to recover.

LCI ran a number of creative educational events, often organised in partnership with others, which was where my educational experience came into its own. Three events drew on the *Faithful Cities* report to explore aspects of poverty, race and faith within the city, using a variety of learning styles including art, music and drama. Over the years, I had worked with another colleague to explore the theme of 'Making a Good City'; this I wrote up in an accessible style and it was distributed to all the city councillors.[11]

Other events drew on aspects of community theatre, two of which took place in Leeds Parish Church (now Leeds Minster). One celebrated the granting of a charter to the city, and another explored aspects of Herod's life. A third was run in another city-centre venue to develop and enact a series of myths and stories from across the world. These all attracted younger people and ensured that LCI was better known as a creative and exploratory learning organisation, willing to develop work with a wide diversity of ages and beliefs.

I was also asked to tutor several modules on mission and ministry on the Lay Readers' course and be part of a team assessing the work of curates in the diocese. I learned much from the African Caribbean community when we were jointly running a series of church-based events in the city to celebrate the two-hundredth anniversary of the abolition of transatlantic slavery. The music that inspired me most was the spiritual 'Steal Away

---

[11] Margaret Halsey and Nigel Greenwood, *Making a Good City: Reflections on Urban Life and Faith in Leeds* (Leeds: Leeds Church Institute, 2010).

to Jesus' and the steel band whose members had initiated and developed the Leeds carnival.

In my last year in post we had established a regular annual lecture in memory of our founder Walter Hook, sponsored by LCI, Leeds Minster and the university religious studies department. The first lecture was given by Dame Mary Warnock, and the second by Professor Mona Siddiqui. My biggest delight was when we had commissioned a poem by Carol Ann Duffy as a gift to mark the making of Leeds Minster. When she came to read it, the place was packed out. When I retired six months later I had given as much as possible to the post, which had been stretching, challenging and ultimately satisfying.

When I left work, I returned to the ritual group to privately mark the transition. As two of us retired at the same time, we could explore aspects of the transition together. We used some weighing scales, counterbalancing the gains and losses of the experience, which for each of us had been different. As there was no longer a notice on our office doors, the group produced new notices for each of us where others had written what they had heard about our achievements on labels shaped like slices of watermelon. I returned home to Leeds with this, and with a gold goblet containing a golden candle.

My employment in Brighton, Sheffield, Manchester and Leeds went against the grain of structural clericalism and sexism, where it had often been taken for granted that ordained people had authority over lay people, and men over women. The assumptions made it hard to develop a more collaborative and creative style of teamwork, and at times I had found it very stressful. Sometimes I had felt as if I was walking a tightrope between different world views, at others as if I was steering a small ship in stormy waters, and at others as if I was part of a kaleidoscope waiting for the pieces to fall into a different place.

Who can find a virtuous woman?

However, my small affectionate house rabbit provided regular company and took me out of myself as she enjoyed her dandelion leaves and carrots. So the Easter hymn I would currently choose would be 'Now the Green Blade Rises from the Buried Grain'.

Some theologians describe Easter as the eighth day of creation, explored by Ann Lewin in her poem 'After word':

> Thus heavens and earth were
> Finished, and were good. But
> In the middle of the night, God woke.
> 'It might be burdensome,' he thought,
> 'To give dominion over all created things
> To earthling folk: lest they should
> Take themselves too seriously,
> I'll give them music and a
> Sense of fun, to lighten duty and
> Enliven praise.'
> So in wise mercy did Creator God.
> And all the seventh day, he rested,
> Well content.[12]

---

[12] 'After word' from *Watching for the Kingfisher* by Ann Lewin is © Ann Lewin, 2009. Published by Canterbury Press. Used by permission. rights@hymnsam.co.uk

9.
In and out of the church

Maggie Butcher

I entered the church screaming and there have been times when I've felt I might leave the same way. I began writing this after reading that the Church of England had said once again, and for what seems the umpteenth time, that sex is for married heterosexual couples only. I did not and do not intend this piece to focus on the Church of England's to me inane and deeply hurtful, not to say ostrich-like, attitude to sexuality, but such utterances only make me ask myself what makes me stay in a church many of whose pronouncements and practices I find either irrelevant or deeply offensive. But, by the time I finished, the landscape had changed so utterly because of COVID-19. I have seen and experienced church in ways that can only make me feel humble and blessed to consider myself part of it.

Unlike some of the other contributors to this volume, I have never held a professional or paid position within the church but have been a sitter in the pew for most of my life, albeit a critical one, and have been and still am active in a number of roles. I realise that as an elderly married woman I represent perhaps the image of a typical middle-class churchgoer so alien to many people in twenty-first-century England, but would like to suggest that appearances can be deceptive. I explore in this piece something of my own personal history within the church and what it is that keeps me in it when my faith is at best of the wavering kind, and my desire still in some churches simply to get up and leave is quite strong.

I was baptised into the Anglican fold at 6 months old in May 1947 when the exceptionally hard winter that year, with its heavy snowfall, had finally abated, permitting my mother to get my pram out of the house and wheel it the mile or so up to St Michael's Church, Woburn Sands. Several other babies of that early post-war baby boom were christened with me but as a child I was never allowed to forget that no one in the church heard anything of the service on account of my unremitting caterwauling. The church archives have a picture of me a few months later, scowling as I was handed over to the then incumbent, the Revd Fred Bowler, at some church gathering, perhaps a meeting of the Mothers' Union where my mother was eventually to become the Enrolling Member, chairing and organising the monthly meeting.

Going to church was an important part of our lives. My mother and I were regular attenders at the 9.15 Communion Service but I do not recall my father, who was terminally ill and died when I was 8, ever coming with us. On Sunday afternoons I joined Miss Hebbes' little crocodile of infants from Chapel Street, past the Methodist church, along the High Street to the Ellen Pettit Memorial Hall for Sunday school. We all began in Miss Hebbes' class, docilely submitting to her strict discipline, where we learnt to sing 'Jesus Bids Us Shine'– with all the requisite gestures – in our own 'small corner', where our 'pure, clear light' would, we fervently hoped, shine out 'like a little candle burning in the night'.

Edgewise?

I generally enjoyed Sunday school, where the then vicar, Michael Meakin, at that time something of an Anglo-Catholic, taught us as we grew older about vestments and saints and showed us, in those largely pre-television days, films of the natural world. Women from the congregation were our class teachers, and as a young teenager I was recruited into their ranks. Around the age of 13 I had been confirmed, after attending confirmation preparation. Perhaps there were group meetings for those of us about to be confirmed but all I remember was the individual one-to-one session with Mr Meakin in the Lady Chapel in an otherwise unlit and chilly church one dark evening. I felt distinctly uncomfortable, not least because I was aware that Mr Meakin knew rather more about me than most of the other candidates and was probing too deeply for my comfort into areas of my life at home that I preferred to keep hidden. During my father's illness I was frequently sent to the vicarage, where I played with the two Meakin daughters, both a little younger than me. Mr Meakin encouraged me, giving me books such as Mrs Gaskell's *Cranford* and talking to me about books by Alan Paton and Boris Pasternak. While my mother did the cleaning for Mrs Meakin, I helped him to redecorate the vast Georgian farmhouse that was then the vicarage, pasting rolls of paper and holding the plumb line as he papered the walls. Mr Meakin was a fine calligrapher and also had a printing press, and I enjoyed folding and binding the material he produced for church.

Nevertheless, by the time I was 15 or thereabouts I was beginning to rebel. I found the services stuffy and repetitive, and was reprimanded by Mr Meakin for not attending. But I was learning Greek at school and Mr Enoch, my grammar school teacher, had bought me a Greek New Testament, so on my infrequent visits I would follow the lessons and Gospel in that, pretension winning out over piety every time.

Meanwhile, at school, we had a Student Christian Movement (SCM) group, which met once a week in the lunch hour. I think I might have started it along with a friend from my village who belonged to the Plymouth Brethren. I know that I thought we should invite speakers to our lunchtime meetings and that I took it upon myself to write to the only people I and my friends knew, namely local clergy from Bletchley and the neighbouring villages. I remember Mr Wigg from Wavendon came with his handbells, but what Mr Hedley from Bletchley, or the Rector of Fenny Stratford, or even the lone deaconess who rejoiced in the name of Petronella, imparted to us has left no trace in my memory, nor what we got up to in the absence of such visitors. I do recall, however, that one of my teachers, the rotund cleric, the Revd Leslie Garrett, warned me against creating what he called 'a holy huddle'. Of course, at the time I didn't fully understand what he meant. I remember him with affection, not just for the glowing end-of-school report he gave me, but for teaching me how to overcome my slight stammer and to project my voice to be able to read in public.

The best thing about SCM so far as I was concerned was that the central organisation, which was very active in schools and universities in the late 1950s and 60s, and was of a more liberal cast than the evangelical Christian Union, organised summer work parties, which were advertised in a booklet on our school noticeboard. Open to school students over the age of 16, they offered two-week holidays in conjunction with established projects, working for example with the elderly, disabled young people or disadvantaged children in different parts of the country. I read of a project based in a community centre for old men in Aberdeen that appealed to me, for reasons that are now unclear. Perhaps it was simply that Aberdeen was so far away. My friend Beth, a year older than me and in a higher form, said she would come with me. The problem was I was only 15. Somehow, the rules were bent – a letter from my ever-complaisant headmaster perhaps? – and I went. I remember we took our sleeping bags and slept on straw palliasses in a makeshift dormitory in the St Katherine's Centre, and that we spent our first day chatting to the old men over mugs of strong tea. The main difficulty was in understanding what they were saying and making ourselves understood. One old chap sat me down and patiently and slowly told me in his thick Aberdonian accent that I'd surely heard of missionaries being sent to China; they should send them south to England too. Perhaps he was more aware than I at the time how irksome being done good to can be for the supposed beneficiary.

I went on a couple more such working parties and it was at one of them that I met two women, Glenda Jones and Brenda Mawby, both teachers, who, besides rescuing me from an over-zealous room-mate's earnest prayers and reading aloud of 1 Timothy every night, told me about William Temple College in Rugby where they were then studying. The college trained lay men and women from industry, the civil service, social work and education to relate Christian faith to the realities of the secular world. Knowing that I had by then completed two years in the sixth form at school and was staying on for one more term to try for Oxbridge, they suggested I write to the Principal, Miss Mollie Batten, asking if I might then spend the next two terms at the college as a kind of au pair.

I recall with some embarrassment regaling the redoubtable Miss Batten at interview with my conviction that Quakerism was far preferable to the C of E. She nodded sagely as she puffed on her pipe and told me she would accept me, on condition that as well as helping in the kitchen, as previous au pairs had done, I would also study alongside the other students, attending seminars and tutorials and taking the same classes as them in Christian doctrine, biblical studies, sociology and, in my case, New Testament Greek as well. I was eager to begin, and thought that was all I needed to know, but she looked at me sternly and told me that I had failed to ask crucial questions as to what remuneration I should expect and how I intended to live without income: a salutary lesson in workers' rights and practical Christianity! I would, she explained, get my board, lodging and tuition free, but would receive what I thought the princely sum of £2 a week to cover my personal expenses, which it did quite adequately.

As an introduction to university life, the opportunity to attend lectures and seminars, with the luxury of individual tutorials with the eminent but wonderfully genial Leonard Hodgson, formerly Regius Professor of Divinity at Oxford, then – although I did not know it at the time – in his last year of life, was unparalleled. I do not recall the essay topics he set for me but I do remember his remarking that he had not seen Milton quoted before in any undergraduate essay he had ever read. Dr Hodgson, an erstwhile suitor of Dorothy L. Sayers, reminded me very much of my grandfather and I felt a great rapport with him. I remember laughing at his telling me how once when preaching on the book of Revelation and referring to 'the lake which burneth with fire and brimstone', he had got carried away and amused the congregation with his reference to 'brimstone and treacle', then an old remedy for aches and pains, and not the title of a controversial Dennis Potter play, which came some years later.

I have no recollection of attending church at Rugby, beyond occasional Sunday morning visits to the new Coventry Cathedral, consecrated only some three years earlier, which with its arresting Graham Sutherland tapestry, vivid stained glass and John Piper glass doors, excited my visual imagination: one entered to what seemed a blaze of light and colour, and against such a backdrop, the liturgy, while formal, possessed a sense of drama and purposefulness, imbued as it was with a sense of hope and the desire for renewal after the devastation of war.

My companions on such visits were likely to be my fellow students, all of whom were at least a decade older than me, if not considerably more. One such was an Australian, Margery Chisholm, who worked for the Bishop of Melbourne. She was, it strikes me, much the same age as I am now, and it has taken me all this time to understand much of what she was trying to tell me then, to hold lightly to theoretical belief and dogma and instead to see divine purpose and presence in a cosmic understanding of Christian spirituality. She took me under her wing, and did her best, through simple yoga exercises and meditation, to show a lumpy provincial girl how to be and how to live in her body, something it has taken me the best part of a lifetime fully to appreciate.

I had no contact with church beyond college chapel during my time at King's College, London, but as King's offered all its students, not just those studying theology, the opportunity to study for its Associate of King's College (AKC) diploma, I took Geoffrey Parrinder's course in comparative religion alongside my degree in English. It was a subject I was already interested in and certainly proved helpful when I went as a volunteer with VSO to Sokoto in the north of Nigeria in late 1968 to teach, the only woman and the only non-Muslim, at the Arabic Teachers' College there. I had read the Qur'an and was familiar at least with the basic tenets of Islam, if not the particular forms it took in that part of the world.

In September 1974 I returned to Nigeria to take up a

position at Ahmadu Bello University in Zaria. There was a strong evangelical Christian presence on campus and I had colleagues, both expatriate and Nigerian, who were firmly committed to it but I stayed resolutely away, as much for reasons linked to my first sojourn in that country as to prejudice against evangelical Christianity. In 1969 I had become engaged to be married to one of my Nigerian Muslim colleagues in Sokoto. We spent time together in Leeds where I had gone to teach and where I took an MA in Commonwealth Literature at the university. On return to Nigeria we quickly realised marriage was not on the cards but I felt a strong bond of loyalty, both to him and to my Muslim erstwhile colleagues, so as not to be seen to be rushing into a church for which I had no particular sympathy and to which I'd shown no inclination before. Nevertheless, when I went hitchhiking in the vacations by myself I would have with me names and addresses given to me by my colleagues, of for example mission schools, including one where I stayed in the north-east of the country now suffering from the depredations of Boko Haram.

It was only in Canada, where I had gone directly from Nigeria in 1976, to do a PhD at the University of Saskatchewan in Saskatoon, that I returned to the church, once again via the university chaplaincy, at a time of stress, if not to say crisis, in my life. I knew I needed to speak with someone, and I was adamant that it should not be the genial university chaplain himself, Colin Clay, who became a personal friend. He quite properly suggested another priest, someone who later became a bishop in the Anglican Church of Canada. Under his direction, I made a formal confession, a valuable and perhaps not much talked about rite within Anglicanism. I found it immensely moving, profound and ultimately liberating, and wish it were perhaps more widely known.

Edgewise?

Colin was a powerful anti-nuclear advocate and a wise pastor. Not without personal difficulties and upheavals in his own life, he knew how to reach out to others in pain, be they churchgoers or not. One of the professors in my department, with no Christian or other religious faith, suffered the horrendous experience of losing a son in a house fire. Colin took the young man's funeral but then simply took time regularly to go fishing with the grieving father in one of the lakes north of the city. Their surplus catch of fearsomely bony pike would often end up in a bucket outside my front door. That kind of practical, undemonstrative living out of the gospels appealed to me, along with a sense that unless Christianity is about community and social justice and openness it is merely empty words. I found meaning and solace in becoming part of a worshipping community on campus, although I never disclosed then or later what had brought me there. I sometimes invited to come along with me the elderly, English-born GP who was the senior medical officer to the university and my wise and understanding confidante. 'You know, Maggie,' Liz would say, 'I don't really believe in all this, but while I'm here I almost think I do': a sentiment that I understand and that speaks to me in my more sceptical moments. But the Anglican liturgy, and especially the Eucharist, speaks to me powerfully of inclusiveness and forgiveness, while the rhythm of the church year is comfortingly familiar and supportive, providing a context and framework for daily life and growth.

When I returned to London in 1980 to work at the Commonwealth Institute, my meeting with the man who would become my first husband took me to St Martin-in-the-Fields, which had then, as it has still, a strong internationalist outlook and social commitment to the homeless and those on the margins. We both served on the PCC and I was also a representative on Deanery Synod; I even put myself forward as a candidate, unsuccessfully as it turned out, for General Synod. But I grew increasingly restive. It was bad enough that, although we were regular and committed churchgoers, the then vicar refused to allow us to be married in church as my husband had earlier been divorced. We were obliged to marry in a register office and have a blessing in church in the course of the Sunday morning Eucharist. We, and certainly family members, were unprepared for the sermon, delivered from on high from the pulpit, which pointed out my husband's shortcomings – but interestingly not mine – in no uncertain way. If it was meant to be humorous it missed the mark by a long shot.

I joined the Movement for the Ordination of Women (MOW) and attended its meetings and rallies. In my studies in Canada I had read extensively in women's colonial and post-colonial literature and regarded myself – how could I not? – as a feminist, albeit of a fairly moderate persuasion. It was disconcerting to say the least to find myself, in what regarded itself as a progressive church, branded a radical feminist merely for raising the need for inclusive language in the liturgy. A favourite prayer of one of the churchwardens began, 'I am two men', which by no stretch of the imagination could include at least half the congregation. My efforts fell, if not on deaf ears, at least on ones disinclined to take the matter seriously. 'I have no problem at all being referred to as "man"' was a refrain I heard often. I was glad that Hannah Ward and Jennifer Wild had by then published, with Janet Morley, their book *Celebrating Women*, a collection of prayers and readings for personal and group worship. Hannah and Jennifer ran a monthly women's group, which I began to attend, and they bravely accepted an invitation to run a Lent course at St Martin's. I think it was Hannah who said it was rather like hitting one's head against a brick wall. Still, I persevered at St Martin's. Mine was not a lone voice, although it sometimes felt that way. My husband and I were branded 'difficult', but things came to a head the Sunday following General Synod's decision in 1992 to allow the ordination of women to the priesthood. I came into church and saw a friend sitting at the front who turned to me and called out, 'Yippee!' The Vicar approached me and said in no uncertain terms, 'We'll have no triumphalism here.' What should have been a day of rejoicing in a church that nominally supported women's ordination was oddly and quite deliberately muted. I've never had a vocation to the priesthood myself but I know the hurt and frustration of those who did and wanted their long waiting, and our support, to be celebrated.

As a result of my estrangement from St Martin's and, as it turned out, growing estrangement in our marriage, I started going to St James's Piccadilly, then with Donald Reeves as rector. Compared with St Martin's, it was at that time administratively a rather chaotic place, but one where women's ministry was enthusiastically endorsed. Ulla Monberg, then a deacon there, was among the first group of women to be ordained and there was much celebration of that event. At that time, St James's revelled, sometimes overmuch in my view, in its sense of being different from its staider church neighbours, but it certainly encouraged and promoted inclusivity in language and innovative liturgy. Donald instigated the practice of the whole congregation encircling the altar for communion, which continued through the incumbency of Charles Hedley (son of the rector whom I invited to my school so long ago!) to the present, with Lucy Winkett, our rector for more than a decade. It is for me, as for many, a powerful and moving symbol of openness and welcome, where all, regardless of background and social standing, age, gender or sexuality, meet not as lone individuals but as illustration of the infinite variety of God's people in thankfulness for our common life. We receive the elements of bread and wine, and the clergy and servers take the sacrament last, serving each other after they have served everyone else, a practice I find profoundly symbolic of the relationship between clergy and community and, for me, more resonant than Maundy Thursday foot-washing, though obviously based on a similar principle. And at St James's it is not only clergy who do the washing but churchwardens too.

I have now been attending St James's for more than a quarter of a century and consider it, as do so many others, my spiritual home. Over the years I have served on several PCCs, including a stint as lay chair. We describe ourselves on our website as being a church that is inclusive, welcoming and adventurous, which is, I think, a fair summary of who and where we are, but I would also add self-questioning, and cognisant of the issues that face churches with a considerable national and international profile. We have in Lucy Winkett a rector well known for her broadcasting, and certainly enjoy a quality of preaching from her and the rest of our clergy team that is perhaps uncommon. Because of our position in central London we can, for example, host public debates and engage with urgent social issues more readily than some other parishes in less privileged positions.

The creation of a replica of the infamous Bethlehem Wall in front of the church at Christmas 2016, through which everyone wishing to enter the church had to pass, certainly made the headlines and caused no little controversy. It is probably true to say that we had underestimated the amount of vitriol levelled at the Rector in particular, but, with support from church members, she weathered the worst of it. I think the whole community thought the exercise worthwhile in bringing to the fore, through performances, debates and discussion, shared meals and shared experiences, the grim reality of life for the Palestinian people for whom the Wall is an ever-present reality affecting every aspect of their lives within Israel. The breaking down of the wall with an irruption of dance and song on Twelfth Night was a potent symbol of hope yet to be enacted in that divided country.

Since then the renowned war artist Arabella Dorfman has created two moving installations in the church deriving from her time spent on the Greek island of Lesbos working alongside refugees. The first, in 2015/16, *Flight*, consisted of a small orange dinghy suspended above the nave, one of many discarded and left on the shore after its occupants had made their treacherous journey across the Mediterranean. Who knows how many occupants it held or whether they all reached safety?

In 2017/18 many church members helped Arabella construct *Suspended*, an illuminated and constantly moving assemblage of clothes similarly discarded or simply lost on the beach as their refugee owners scrambled ashore. No one who saw this enormous construction high above their heads could fail to be moved by the single child's shoe, the tiny dresses, the T-shirts and little dungarees. To whom did they once belong? What happened to them? In such dramatic ways are brought home to us the stark reality of the dispossessed, the human 'collateral' of conflict and war.

But St James's is still a parish church, with all that that entails. The parish might include some of the wealthiest thoroughfares in London, with high-end shops, exclusive clubs and hedge-fund managers as neighbours, but there are many people without homes living rough on those same streets who daily sleep in the church pews or are guests at our winter shelter. I am clerk to a small charity administered by the church that provides a small quarterly stipend to needy persons living in our Westminster borough. Several refugees and present and past asylum seekers attend our Saturday morning breakfasts and are supported by a large number of volunteers, from within and outside our worshipping community, including members of the East London Mosque, with whom we've regularly shared an iftar meal in church at the end of Ramadan. Our last Christmas Day lunch was attended by some 120 people, many of whom were provided with transport by members of the West London Synagogue who also helped in the mammoth task of preparing and cooking the meal.

So far so good, but other inner-city churches with a 'gathered' congregation – that is to say, drawn from a wide area and not themselves resident in the parish – are engaged in no less. What I find particularly encouraging about SJP, which is perhaps less easily discoverable in other churches, is that these activities are not always clergy-driven and do not depend on being clergy-led. We are blessed with a great many talented and able people in the community whose gifts are encouraged and developed through the very many groups and activities on offer; some even find themselves in possession of talents they did not know they had. A monthly half-hour of silent prayer, in pre-COVID times held after the morning Eucharist, is generally led by a member of the clergy team, but not exclusively so, and a member of the community researches and provides the two daily short readings that are available in printed form and online for those who make this their daily practice. Similarly, the Camino course, a regular programme of discovering and learning more about the various aspects of Christian faith, which normally runs from Advent to Ascension Day and is offered to both newcomers and to those of us long in the pews, has a large input from its lay leaders. Our Eco-church activities, for which we have reached gold standard, were the initiative of lay persons, including a scientist churchwarden, and have radically altered the consumption of energy on site and attitudes to conservation and waste, and reach out to and influence the wider congregation in their awareness of how such measures are a practical demonstration of their concern and responsibility as Christians for the environment and the planet. Underpinned by talks, workshops, sermons and a monthly garden eco-liturgy, they make theology real and down to earth.

Perhaps we at St James's take for granted the practice of inviting anyone who wishes to give a notice before the final hymn to do so, provided they are not repeating something already noted in the service sheet and do not last longer than 30 seconds. Of course not everyone adheres to the rule and some political hobby horses occasionally get ridden (to not always inward groans), but few of us realise what a novelty it is when notices elsewhere are generally only given by the clergy.

This is of a piece with the attitude of the clergy to questions such as, 'Why don't we do this?' or 'Why don't we have so and so?' The response more likely than not is, 'Well, why don't you try it?' Initiatives such as the Animal Welfare Group started in this way, as have several others. Our pastoral assistants have, over the past few years, been assiduous in helping build up the twenties and thirties group. They enjoy a monthly space called Circus Spirit on Sunday afternoons, as part of the varied Sunday afternoon and evening Sunday Spirit series, but are fully integrated into the rest of church life, some as intercessors, servers and readers; some with supporting asylum seekers, with LGBTQ+ activities, London Citizens and more.

If getting to know everyone in such a diverse and scattered community Sunday by Sunday can be a challenge, fairly frequent community lunches served in church after the service help, as do newcomers' lunches, lunches organised by the LGBTQ+ Group and open to all, and invitations to volunteer help in myriad ways, from the Fairtrade stall and selling eggs from retired ex-battery hens to joining in counting the birds in the garden or serving coffee. If eating and drinking figure quite largely in church life it is quite deliberate: we say we are called to God's inexhaustible banquet and wish to see everyone invited and welcomed to it.

And now in these days, weeks and months of separation and distancing because of COVID-19, and when the church building, like all other places of worship and meeting, has only recently reopened for limited socially distanced worship with limited numbers, we find ourselves seeking new ways to connect with each other and beyond. Sunday services and a midday office, 'Holding the Silence', are being live-streamed, and the Camino group's Wednesday Eucharist has continued past Ascension Day via Zoom, with members of the group reading the lesson and Gospel (indeed lay persons always read the Gospel on Sundays too) and offering their own 'gospel' by way of a story from their own life over the preceding week. Other groups are contacting their members by various forms of social media or by phone, and new cluster groups based largely on locality have been set up with the aim of providing support and a listening ear to those who might need it or have asked to be included. One group says Compline every evening via Zoom, another reads all four gospels day by day. Some of us have joined in the daily morning 'Reboot' offered by our new associate rector, which combines yoga and meditation, and might continue in some form after the pandemic has become history. Perhaps as never before it has been brought home to us that church isn't necessarily, or even at all, a place where we go but rather who we are, daily attempting to live our lives modelled on the Christ who calls us and in whose light we minister to each other: candle flames in a world that can seem at times very dark.

10.
Openings

Jennifer Wild

Lay woman. What do these words conjure up in your mind? 'Lay man' is another matter – until women were ordained in the diaconate and then priesthood in the Anglican Church, 'lay man' could be said to cover everyone else, although 'lay person' and even 'lay woman' no doubt were sometimes used. But my guess is that 'lay woman' came to the fore in England in 1992, and for nearly twenty years of the twenty-first century the contributors to this book were among a group who gathered annually as lay women. When we were considering the possibility of the book my partner asked me, 'What does the expression "lay woman" mean to you?' And without stopping to think I said, 'Freedom'. What follows is an attempt to find out and write down something of what I meant.

In the New Zealand summer, the sun (on the whole) shines, the garden greens, the sea is friendly. In the year I was born, far away in Germany there is a new Chancellor, Adolf Hitler, but here at home life goes on. Our father had seen only the tail end of the Great War, and by the time the next Great War began he was past the age for call-up. In New Zealand after Pearl Harbour and the fall of Singapore, the nearer threat was the Japanese advance south and round the Pacific. We no longer holidayed at Waikanae on the coast north-west of Wellington. In fact the coastline there was fenced in barbed wire to entangle any hostile approach. The nearest war came to those who were the young children of our household in the early 1940s was in the aftermath of one of the 1942 earthquakes, when the family lavatory suffered a cracked bowl and had to be used with anxious care for some months, if not years, because the country's economy was concentrated on 'the war effort', and various home comforts were not available for the time being. American troops stationed in NZ before some of the fiercest phases of the war in the Pacific led to my mother one day finding all her tulip flowers decking the body of a GI who was 'playing dead' on the grass outside our fence, and encouraging the neighbourhood kids to decorate his corpse. My mother had to bite her lips and keep silence – so many of them did die, without benefit of tulips.

Our river valley was not suited for the type of air-raid shelters that householders were encouraged to dig in their gardens – the level of the water table rose sharply if any rain fell at all, and no one minded that in fact we never needed to make use of our shelter except for rather damp fun. We young ones just carried on growing and putting up with the rather crabby (we thought) married women who came back to teaching to fill the gaps left by departing troops or conscientious objectors. The country's young were not to be left in the care of the latter, but Mrs Grumble and her successors were perhaps used to a more tightly controlled atmosphere in the classroom.

The year 1877 saw NZ's defining educational legislation, at least for pakeha (Europeans). Education offered by the state was to be free, compulsory and secular. And indeed it was. Somewhere back in the first half of the nineteenth century my father's great grandfather found success and (comparative) wealth in the heyday of Britain's trade in cotton, centred on Manchester, where he also found a new lease of spiritual life in the teachings of Swedenborg.

Neither business nor prosperity far outlasted him, what with the Crimean war and civil war in the USA, and the quarrelsomeness of some of a later generation of his family in the New Church. His grandson, my grandfather, migrated to New Zealand as a young man. Once there, he fairly soon completed training as a teacher and acquired the reputation in the family of having taught in every one-teacher school in Southland by the time he retired, having barely set foot outside NZ's most southerly province.

After my father's war service he was awarded a grant that enabled him to complete a BSc degree in Edinburgh, before returning to NZ and a teaching job in a rural secondary school where one of his brothers was the founding headmaster, and where Dad met our mother. My father's acquaintance with religious practice seems to have very nearly fizzled out in his boyhood after he was either cast out of the local church choir or told to sing very quietly. Not very encouraging. As far as I could make out, he did not venture into any church during his years in Edinburgh.

My mother had grown up in a much more explicitly Christian environment: her father (as far as I can glean) was a free spirit in a definitely Protestant tradition, emphatically not what he called a 'man-worshipper' (referring perhaps to the deference paid to rather pretentious 'elders' visiting from the home country), and far too literally 'temperate' to approve of teetotalism. My maternal grandmother, on the other hand, found her place with the Plymouth Brethren's teaching and practice, though in its slightly freer stage – she landed up 50-odd miles from the nearest 'meeting' in NZ, but remained 'in fellowship' with its members for the rest of her life. As seen through my mother's eyes, Grandma was in her own way a 'free spirit'. My main encounter with her, within a month or so of her death, was when she was staying with us, and every day I sat on her lap while she read me a chapter of

Matthew's gospel. All I remember is a degree of argument when Grandma said she'd skip the 'begats'. Yet in my memory she is the most naturally religious person I have ever known. Warm-hearted and sensible, she seems to me much bigger than all her beliefs. Would that we all were. My mother's memories filled out my picture of life in their household. A slightly impatient call to 'Come and give thanks 'cos it's cheese!' enfolds gratitude to God the provider with respect for the cook's hot dish, which must not be allowed to get cool and thence tough.

So, what was the inheritance of my generation in New Zealand? There was, it seems to me, a bare acceptance of some undefined religious patterns of thought relating to the Christian tradition and its story. Perhaps my eyes began to be opened by the fact that although SCM in the immediate post-war days did work in some state schools (on an entirely voluntary basis and not in official classroom terms), of the 700–800 pupils at our secondary school the SCM group was never larger than about eight to twelve pupils and one or two staff.

At university, at first I joined the SCM group (this was just before SCM's more political days), where my memories are of the smell of lunchtime sandwiches accompanying rather strained discussion of (for example) whether belief in the Virgin Birth was necessary for salvation. Perhaps these were the questions of the time, especially for those entering adulthood and, as university students, being confronted with questions to ponder and argue about rather than facts to memorise. Be that as it may, because some of my friends were active Baptists I began to attend some Evangelical Union gatherings, where the theology seemed carefully confident, though I always fell foul of the expectation that we would all be involved in 'personal work' with the unbelievers around us. In retrospect I suspect that Christian belief in the generally Protestant-coloured part of New Zealand's

Christian population was slipping away rather fast into ignorance and indifference. Was it cowardice to be relieved in my last years at university at the inauguration of an Anglican Society? I think this was the first time I sensed that some of us wanted or needed to examine our collective history in our many-layered denomination.

And so (in 1956) to Britain, England and Cambridge, and a taste of Anglicanism in its own territory, so to speak, where a lot could be taken for granted, and the Franciscan spirit further enlivened the congregation of St Benet's. Lucky me.

∽

What has happened to Christian faith as a public matter, that is, one where everyone is involved? First, who is this 'everyone'? As nations and societies we have learned something (and clearly the learning has to go on) about respecting the beliefs and faiths of others, not just in the various communities of Christians, not just in those of monotheistic religions, or of non-theistic or even anti-religious beliefs. Respect, yes. But how public is public? Within the range of Christian groups there are some whose enactment of their faith in worship is full of song and sound and movement, others who practise a collective and silent waiting on God, others whose worship is expressed in orderly and often magnificent liturgy, and for others in passionate preaching and response to it in hymn-singing or other music-making. Anglicanism may express itself in any of these ways (except, perhaps, in silence). And to cap that, it can claim reticence as its birthmark – witness Queen Elizabeth I's reluctance to 'make windows into men's souls'. This runs two ways, though: reticence might work when everyone knows where they are, what they are to do, why they are to do it, what they are a part of. Scratch the surface, however, and what appears often seems an amazing unawareness, a kind of lifelong immaturity increasingly lapsing into ignorance. Since this writer's teens, the ingredient missing from what is (or was) offered to children attending Sunday school or the like is a real religious education, all the more necessary as the general retreat into religious privacy produces new generations of religious ignorance – and, at the same time, an inevitable decline in religious adherence.

No doubt this gives a rather shallow and inadequate account of mid-twentieth-century Protestant Christian practice and sensitivities in Britain. As a teenager in New Zealand I recognised in myself what seemed a rather shameful embarrassment at the thought of professing 'my' Christian faith out loud, as some of my Baptist friends were happy to do. Any public confession of faith (I might have admitted) would be more easily managed as a sort of mantelpiece ornament – something always there, dusted or polished when necessary but seldom explicitly mentioned.

I think that in the short run the Franciscans in Cambridge contributed much to let me enter a world of greater freedom both to speak and to share a silence that was embedded in a kind of companionship in faith. It dawned on me that there was a way of life that seemed like home in the sense of a starting place.

There were two years of study followed by three years discovering that I was definitely not cut out to be an academic, before I asked to join the Community of St Clare as the place to live out what I had been given.

In nearly twenty-seven years of contemplative life in community, what did I learn? It is probably a waste of time to attempt a full answer to that question, but along with quite a bit of gardening and cooking and housework and learning and relearning to breathe, and pondering what 'standing before God with the mind in the heart' might mean in practical terms,

I did learn a little about living with other people. My parents (especially my mother, who was the thirteenth of her family) had always impressed on us that they had four individual children – we were not just a collection of two adults and a batch of four kids. The obvious truth of that was a big help when reflecting on the fact that I had opted, and been accepted, to live in another sort of family of individuals who did not grow up and go their separate ways, but had each solemnly undertaken to spend the whole remainder of their life together. It was possible to learn not to obsess on this, but I have never taken easily to 'family' talk applied to religious communities, while at the same time felt closer in some weird way to my siblings and their offspring 12,000 miles away. And if someone says, 'Absence makes the heart grow fonder', I'm happy to retort 'So much the better'.

A sister once said to me: 'This is a truly ordinary life that we are living here.' You could say that that sounds like a thoroughly boring way of passing the time. But I knew what she meant. We carried out household and outdoor tasks to the best of our ability. We seldom went outside the convent premises except for medical or other necessary business. And every day was shaped by the Divine Office. For much of my community life we used a somewhat dated version of the Benedictine office, and although that was later ousted by more modern and shorter offices, a framework for the day remained. I secretly thought the Benedictine-cum-Franciscan versions captured something really appropriate for British Anglican Clares. But an unchanging world in such a matter is neither possible nor (mostly) desirable.

And anyway, I did not stay in the community for the rest of my life after all, and am somehow still alive over thirty years after leaving. Hindu thought, it is said, postulates four phases of an individual's life: student, householder, retired person or hermit, and finally a phase of complete renunciation, when a person is detached from everything but devotion to the divine. One of the history lecturers of my university years in New Zealand, who on his travels had spent time in India, listening to people of wisdom, concluded that Christianity in its entirety was a mere puddle compared to the depths of Hindu thought. At the time I felt some no doubt juvenile indignation at his verdict. But years later, when I had acquired my own sketchy notions of the balance (or not) between the spiritual ways of affirming or denying, the via affirmativa or the via negativa, the kataphatic or the apophatic, the plus or minus of spiritual attitudes and lives, I read a biography of St Francis de Sales, and warmed to the idea that his living out of his faith, his love of God, in the society in which he had been born was as humanly heroic as years of advancing towards naked self-noughting.

When the first women were ordained in the Anglican Church in England, it looked like a great moment, not least because it seemed to leave a space free, after all, to be a lay woman in the C of E. I am not sure that the church knows what that meant, when jobs that used to be done by lay women seem now to be reserved for those who are or who will be ordained. Is it the idea that the clergy are our leaders and lay people by definition are the led? To put this possibility into words is to bring its limitations out into the open. For a long time, priests expected to be (and were regarded as) the public face of the church. If something is missing in those not regarded as leaders, is that why the church's dwindling has gathered speed? Is nothing to be expected of the laity except that they try to be good sheep? It's possible to dispense with any specific metaphor to answer this question, but more than that is needed.

One line of thought runs something like this: for some

women, being the face of the church turned towards the world is experienced in lives lived consciously as service arising from worship and nourished by faith. For a very few, the starting point, the conscious turning towards God, becomes also the place of their response. Hence the religious orders, though by and large neither way of life is flourishing at the moment. For many, the time for religious practice is on the way out, is less thought about, let alone valued, an all but forgotten heritage, although, on the other hand, not a few agnostic, or simply non-religious women live lives that are on the whole intelligently generous, a living rebuke to the merely pious. Maybe for Christian lay women it is becoming ever more important to see that we have a role in restoring and maintaining the flourishing of this planet on which we all live, and that we need to be seen among those making meaningful changes in lifestyle in the face of this most prominent and pressing challenge for humanity at the present time (even during a pandemic).

Perhaps another way of looking for what is needed to find maturity in a Christian life involves looking at suffering, 'the kind of suffering that compels one to act, and thereby produces change', in the words of Dorothee Sölle. She goes on to say:

It is clear that Christianity makes an overwhelming affirmation of suffering, far stronger than many other world views that do not have as their center the symbol of the cross. But this affirmation is only part of the great love for life as a whole that Christians express with the word 'believe'. To be able to believe means to say yes to this life, to this finitude, to work on it and hold it open for the promised future.[1]

---

[1] Dorothy Soelle, *Suffering*, translated by Everett R. Kalin (Philadelphia, PA: Fortress Press, 1975), p. 107.

If the above seems rather too hasty a leap from the everyday to the sublime, I am reminded of a conversation with a Franciscan brother, when he was talking to me about his hopes and fears on making his life vows. He said, 'I took my life in my hands, and felt the better for it.' And this somehow leads me to Augustine's insight:

> If then you are members of the body of Christ, it is the mystery of yourselves that is there on the Lord's table: you receive the mystery of yourselves. You respond 'Amen' to what you are, and in responding you accept to be what you are. You hear the words 'The body of Christ', and you respond 'Amen'. Be a member of the body of Christ that your 'Amen' may prove true.[2]

And at the same time some words from Walter Brueggemann ring true to my understanding: 'Our faith, I propose, is not about pinning down moral certitudes. It is, rather, about openness to wonder and awe in glad praise.'[3]

---

[2] St Augustine of Hippo, from Sermon 272.
[3] Walter Brueggemann, *Mandate to Difference: An Invitation to the Contemporary Church* (Louisville, KY: Westminster John Knox Press, 2007), p. 1.